Annual Publication of
The College Theology Society

A
WORLD MORE HUMAN
A CHURCH
MORE
CHRISTIAN

GEORGE DEVINE
EDITOR-IN-CHIEF

THOMAS McFADDEN   THOMAS L. SHERIDAN, S.J.
MEMBERS OF THE EDITORIAL BOARD

ALBA · HOUSE   alba house   NEW · YORK

A DIVISION OF THE SOCIETY OF ST. PAUL STATEN ISLAND NEW YORK 10314

Nihil Obstat:
Rev. Msgr. William F. Hogan
Censor Librorum

Imprimatur:
+Most Reverend Thomas A. Boland, S.T.D.
Archbishop of Newark
May 18, 1973

The Nihil Obstat and Imprimatur are a declaration that a book or pamphlet is considered to be free from doctrinal or moral error. It is not implied that those who have granted the Nihil Obstat and Imprimatur agree with the contents, opinions or statements expressed.

LIBRARY OF CONGRESS
CATALOGING IN PUBLICATION DATA

College Theology Society.
  A world more human, a church more Christian.

  Proceedings of the national convention of the College Theology Society, held in Los Angeles, Sept. 1-5, 1972.
    Includes bibliographical references.
    1. Theology—Addresses, essays, lectures.
I. Devine, George, 1941-   ed.
II. Title.
BR50.C593   201'.1   73-9512
ISBN 0-8189-0265-5

Current Printing (last digit):
9 8 7 6 5 4 3 2 1

Designed, printed and bound in the United States of America by the Fathers and Brothers of the Society of St. Paul, 2187 Victory Boulevard, Staten Island, N. Y. 10314 as part of their communications apostolate.

TABLE OF CONTENTS

A WORLD MORE HUMAN,
A CHURCH MORE CHRISTIAN

I
INTRODUCTION

The International Congress of Learned Societies in the Field of Religion was impressive in sheer mass alone: when all those in attendance were counted, their number approached two and a half thousand, and they represented fifteen scholarly associations in various areas of religious studies. Most of the societies participating forsook their annual separate meetings, dovetailing them into the congress. Among these was our own College Theology Society, seeking to enjoy the fruits of a "theological common market" with the other groups present, the wisdom of a planeload of European scholars in attendance, and still the distinct identity and autonomy of one's own meeting in tandem with the larger conglomerate.

The theme of the congress, "The Humanizing of Man," was evident in all of the general sessions, and in many of the special sessions given by the various societies, including two sessions which the College Theology Society was pleased to sponsor jointly with the Catholic Theological Society of America. In addition, the particular sessions of each participating association allowed for the development of special interests and individual competencies and approaches. This was evident in the various CTS sessions which manifested a concern for the life of the Catholic theological community, and especially its enterprise as translated into the collegiate classroom. Thus, we have been concerned with the humanizing of man, and also with the ongoing search of the Church to continually become more effective and credible as a presence-in-the-world of Jesus Christ. To both those ends, this volume is offered.

It will be noted that this book (and its immediate predecessor a year ago)[1] cannot be called simply "the Proceedings" of the College Theology Society. This is because, in some instances, not all papers given at a specific CTS convention can appear in one volume (some, indeed, will be "held over" for a later book). In other cases, space allows for the inclusion of other papers, given at regional meetings or otherwise prepared by CTS members, which do not reflect the national annual convention directly but which are representative of the scholarly and pedagogical industry of our membership as a whole. Several such papers will appear in this volume, and will serve to complement those chapters which directly represent the Society's participation in the congress at Los Angeles on September 1-5, 1972.

The editor is indebted to the Board of Directors of the College Theology Society for their constancy of support, especially our officers: Rev. Francis J. Buckley, S.J., of the University of San Francisco, President; Sister Vera Chester, C.S.J., of the College of St. Catherine, Vice-President; Sister M. Gertrude Anne Otis, C.S.C., of Cardinal Cushing College, Secretary; and Prof. Thomas F. Ryan, of Manhattan College, Treasurer. In addition, thanks are in order for the wise counsel offered by editorial board members Prof. Thomas McFadden of St. Joseph's College and Rev. Thomas Sheridan, S.J., of St. Peter's College. Also most supportive of this enterprise were the members of the Society's committee on publications, Prof. Rodger Van Allen, of Villanova University; Prof. Robert G. Kleinhans of St. Xavier College; and Prof. Gerald Pire of Seton Hall University.

Production of this volume was facilitated by and through the firm of H. Reader & Co., New York City, and the staff in the Department of Religious Studies at Seton Hall University, especially Mrs. Margaret Chiang, Miss Laura Waage, and Miss Ann Brady. Also helpful in this regard were Mr. Ralph Villanova and Mrs. Mae Petrone, and without the constant and cheerful assistance

---

1. That They May Live: Theological Reflections on the Quality of Life. Annual Publication of the College Theology Society, ed. George Devine (Staten Island, N.Y.: Alba House, 1972).

of Mr. Tom Grimm, one wonders if this book could have been produced. The physical appearance of this edition is due to the fine work of Alba House, the publishing division of the Society of St. Paul. Special thanks go to Brother Luke Salm, F.S.C., editor of the Proceedings of the Catholic Theological Society of America, for his assistance with this volume.

Finally, and most importantly, the editor thanks those who have been closest to him throughout this project: his wife Joanne and son George.

GEORGE DEVINE

New York City, February 4, 1973.

II

A WORLD MORE HUMAN
The Humanizing of Man
In Contemporary Religious Studies

1 Toward a Theology of Vulnerability: The Liberating Embrace of the Human Condition

BERNARD P. PRUSAK

The age-old question of the meaning of life has become more acute in a technological age. Some wonder if life must remain the gradual process of obedient socialization into one's slot within an inexorable script provided by those who wield control over society. Must life simply be the acceptance of a pre-packaged routine or can it really hold all the wonder of an ongoing, open-ended, creative experiment? Is life an assembly line or a work of art?

Some do not wish to raise such questions since that might confront them with the fact that they are actually missing something—which would threaten the little happiness they have built up for themselves. Why question the meaning of life or admit the possible value of change? We have already been given the answers; besides, as individuals we are powerless. The power of the system is always there threatening and ready to exclude us if we do not conform to established patterns.

It is ironic that even Christians, who supposedly are open to the *eschaton,* are often afraid of anything new. One reason may be the type of spiritual automation we have built into Christianity. We devised the ideal system. For Catholics, sacraments and laws became somewhat like IBM cards fed into computerized Christians. Originally intended to evoke a peak experience, namely, love of God and fellow humanity, Christianity overly lent itself to an easier path and became an established system.[1] Persons

---

1. Cf. Abraham H. Maslow, Religions, Values, and Peak Experiences

imbued with a fear of God kept the minimum of laws and practices and guaranteed the statistical success of a program.[2] Individual morality and institutional conformity to the uniform practices of the group became ideal substitutes for the risky and uncontrollable Spirit of love transforming the world.

A particular image of Jesus supported the spirituality of obedience and conformity which have so long been the hallmark of
Catholic Christianity. Jesus was the God-man who knew the
meaning of all reality. Yet he freely accepted subjection to the
will of his Father who had determined that his Son was to die
upon a cross for our sins. Jesus accepted his cross as we must
accept ours, in obedience. He was uncomplaining, uncritical, and
humble even to his death upon the cross. For that reason he was
rewarded when he reached heaven where the earthly Jesus became
the glorified Christ. Now he sits at the right hand of the Father
waiting for the time when he will judge our obedience to the will
of the Father, as expressed in the commands of those who head
his Church. We must not break the commandments, keep our
passions under control, and follow the pattern dictated by those
who lead us in his name. In that way we too will be rewarded in
heaven.

The *kenosis* of Jesus was interpreted into what almost appears
a prop for institutional order and preservation. Especially since
medieval times, in great part due to the influence of Celtic mon-

---

(New York: Viking Press, 1970), pp. 21-22; Thomas F. O'Dea, **The Sociology
of Religion** (Englewood Cliffs, N. J.: Prentice-Hall, 1966), pp. 36-54.

2. Since its earliest centuries Christianity has been plagued by those
who would emphasize the wrath of God and fear. Tertullian chastized
those who spoke of a God of love. In his eyes only a God of fear could
adequately stimulate moral living: **Against Marcion** 1, 27. Tertullian
seemed oblivious to the words of 1 John 4:18. In 1936 Josef A. Jungmann
alluded to the difficulty of Catholicism become a **traditional confession—**
a pattern of local customs and practices blended with a series of "musts"
and "don'ts." He deplored such a movement away from the Christ-centered
early Church: **The Good News Yesterday and Today** (New York: W. H.
Sadlier, 1962), p. 3. (25th Anniversary Edition of **Die Frobotschaft und
Unsere Glaubensverkundigung**).

asticism upon the continent, the Western Church identified religious life with rules, whether that of the monastery, or that of morality and canon law for the individual. To live as a Christian became identified with a set of practices or a pattern.[3] Any person of faith who experienced difficulty living in total obedience to the will of religious or civil superiors, who were often identical, was reminded to look at Jesus upon the cross and to remember the redemptive value of his suffering. Patience and passive resignation before earthly superiors were theologically recommended by Jesus' obedience to the Father, even to the death of the cross (Philippians 2:6-11). Religion was divorced from any sense of life as an experiment.

Many have rethought the passive dimension of Christianity. Harvey Cox's *Secular City* articulated the reaction against the image of a cosmic puppeteer, a God who pulled our strings so that we conformed to his script.[4] Currently, social ethics, theologies of the world and of liberation are attempting to move beyond a Christianity of attendance and observance. They stress that this world is not simply a testing ground for individual piety or a waiting room for an afterlife. Christianity is a drama that is played out on this side of death.[5] The Way has to do with living and even with conflict.

Any attempts to bring Christianity into closer contact with the secular world are too little and too late for some who have already rejected Christianity as having little or nothing to say

---

3. Cf. Arthur Mirgeler, **Mutations of Western Christianity** (New York: Herder & Herder, 1964), pp. 66-81. Interestingly, it was in the tenth century that the Crucifix became the supreme symbol of Christianity. The poly-chromed crucifix touched the emotions of believers in a very different way than did the earlier emphasis upon the risen Christ of glory. Cf. Kenneth Clark, **Civilisation** (New York: Harper & Row, 1969), p. 29.

4. (New York: Macmillan, 1965).

5. Cf. Johannes B. Metz, **Theology of the World** (New York: Herder & Herder, 1969), pp. 107-155; also Gustaf Aulen, **Christus Victor** (New York: Macmillan, 1961) and **The Drama and the Symbols: A Book on Images of God and the Problems They Raise** (Philadelphia: Fortress Press, 1970), pp. 65-88, 152-153, 170-171, and 196ff.

for life in the world. At the same time such attempts are likewise meeting with resistance from many rank and file Christians who cannot understand them. Contemporary attempts to integrate Christianity and action in the *polis* seem foreign to those who have previously been taught to view religious practice as individual piety, and that as payment on a mortgaged place in heaven, or a premium on anti-hell insurance.

Moved by the conviction that a genuine Christian lifestyle in a time of rapid change should emphasize flexibility and openness to the needs of people, we shall probe the interpretation of an obedient Jesus seemingly embodied in grass roots spirituality.

Did Jesus orient his entire life to the fact that he was to die on the cross? Was his script prepared by the Father and his whole life a fulfillment of the master plan? Where did Jesus stand in regard to the modern dilemma about the meaning of life?

The Jesus who rises from a literal reading of the words of Paul and the gospels might justify a spirituality which interprets life as freely chosen conformity to a pattern from above.[6] Was that really Jesus' message or was it simply the best that the redactors of the gospels could do when they tried to articulate the event of Jesus' death, looking back on it with faith in the resurrection? To put the problem in more precise terms, is the time ripe

---

6. In discussing the idea of obedience unto death W. D. Davies notes that a passive acceptance of death out of loyalty to the revealed will of God was the crown of loyalty to the Torah. Such an idea was in the air in first-century Judaism and played a great part in Rabbinic Judaism. For that reason Paul would have been familiar with that view which saw in martyrdom the supreme act of obedience. "Moreover, we should expect that in his thinking on the Death of Jesus he would apply to it this concept of obedience; the death of the Messiah could have only one meaning for him, it would be the expression of obedience to the demands of God." **Paul and Rabbinic Judaism: Some Rabbinic Elements in Pauline Theology** (New York: Harper & Row Torchbooks, 1967), p. 265. Commenting on our sacerdotalizing of Jesus, Jean-Paul Audet remarks: "We call him the 'high priest' and the 'priest' par excellence, and barely stop short of saying that he was born in order to **die** on the 'altar' of the cross!" **The Gospel Project** (New York: Paulist Press Deus Books, 1969), p. 30.

for a reinterpretation of Jesus' death in a language and spirituality that reflects contemporary insights into God's role in human history?

Contemporary association of personhood with the categories of consciousness and subjectivity has made theologians wonder about Jesus' self-image and human development.[7] Scriptural criticism raises the question whether Jesus expended much time and self-reflection upon the suffering servant motif. That theme and the majority of Jesus' predictions of his death were possibly written into the gospels by writers who expressed the primitive community's *post factum* reflections upon the passion event.[8] Paul's

---

7. Christians have frequently experienced difficulty in maintaining a proper balance between the divinity and humanity of Christ. One interesting example is the Capuchin, Benet of Canfield (1526-1610), who by-passed the humanity of Christ in the original edition of his **Rule of Perfection.** His superiors were alarmed by the omission. As a result the official edition of 1610 sought to restore the humanity of Jesus by adding six chapters on the contemplation of the Passion. An overemphasis on Jesus' divinity was thought to be corrected by condensing his humanity into the Passion. Annihilation, passivity, and depersonalization remained key elements in the abstract school of spirituality. Along with an emphasis on voluntarism such elements influenced the later course of French spirituality which proved quite influential. Cf. Louis Cognet, **Post-Reformation Spirituality** (New York: Hawthorne Books, 1959), pp. 60-62.

8. Those favoring such a position, but with individual variations, are: Günther Bornkamm, **Jesus of Nazareth** (New York: Harper and Row, 1960), pp. 153-168 and 228-229; John Knox, **The Death of Christ** (London: Collins-Fontana Library, 1967- orig. publ. 1958), pp. 59-91, 101-107, and 133-136; C. K. Barrett, "The Background of Mark 10:45," in **New Testament Essays: Studies in Memory of T. W. Manson,** edited by A. J. B. Higgins (Manchester: Manchester University Press, 1959), pp. 1-18; Morna D. Hooker, **Jesus and the Servant,** (London: S.P.C.K., 1959), pp. 45-102, esp. p. 85f. and her study: **The Son of Man in Mark** (Montreal: McGill University Press, 1967), pp. 183-198; H. E. Tödt, **The Son of Man in the Synoptic Tradition** (Philadelphia: Westminster, 1965), pp. 136 and 141-221. (According to Tödt a great deal depends on whether one views Mk. 10:45 as an authentic saying of Jesus. He (pp. 136-137 and 276) relates Mk. 10:45a to Lk. 22:27 and maintains that Mk. 10:45b was a later expansion of verse 45a within the Palestinian Church.); Ferdinand Hahn, **The Titles of Jesus in Christology** (New York and Cleveland: World Publ. Co., 1969), pp. 21-28 and 54-63; Wolfhart Pannenberg, **Jesus: God and Man** (Philadelphia: Westminster, 1968), pp. 245-269; Reginald H. Fuller, **The Foundations of New Testament Christology** (New York: Charles Scribner's Sons,

stress on Christ crucified must be accepted along with the realization that he, unlike John, never experienced the historical Jesus. Death may not have been the working concept which guided Jesus in the living of his earthly ministry.

The gospel's approach to the earthly ministry of Jesus is most important for contemporary spirituality. Despite the diversity in individual passages about Jesus, one characteristic constantly appears: his friendship with sinners and outcasts. In that context Jesus tried to accomplish a mission to which his inner being drew him. He projected a closeness to God and the conviction that God's kingdom was served by everything that he said and did.[9] His words and deeds were effective of that kingdom. In answer to the question, "Are you he who is to come, or shall we look for another?" he responds, "Go and tell John what you hear and see:

1965), pp. 107-108, 115-119, and 151-154; A. J. B. Higgins, **Jesus and the Son of Man** (Philadelphia: Fortress Press, 1965), p. 202; and John Reumann, **Jesus in the Church's Gospels** (London: S.P.C.K., 1970), pp. 267-286. On page 285 Reumann remarks: "One must therefore say that while Jesus did spend himself in serving, it was only later on that his followers rediscovered the words of Isaiah (53) which took on new meaning in light of the actual life lived by Jesus."

Among those favoring the opposite position are: John W. Bowman, **The Intention of Jesus** (Philadelphia: Westminster, 1943), pp. 2 and 126-136; Oscar Cullmann, **The Christology of the New Testament,** revised edition (Philadelphia: Westminster, 1963), pp. 60-82 and 158-164; C. H. Dodd, **According to the Scriptures** (New York: Scribners, 1952), pp. 88-103, 110, and 114f.; W. Zimmerli and J. Jeremias, **The Servant of God** (Naperville, Ill.: Alec R. Allenson, 1965 rev. ed.), pp. 42-44, 60-61, and 88-106; W. G. Kümmel, **Promise and Fulfillment** (Naperville, Ill.: Allenson, 1957), pp. 109-121; T. W. Manson, **The Servant-Messiah: A Study of the Public Ministry of Jesus** (New York: Cambridge University Press, 1953), p. 36; William Manson, **Jesus the Messiah** (Naperville, Ill.: Allenson, 1943), pp. 112 and 117; Vincent Taylor, **The Gospel According to St. Mark** (New York: St. Martin's Press, 1952), p. 122f. and **Jesus and His Sacrifice** (London: Macmillan, 1937), pp. 48 and 282.

9. Cf. E. Käsemann, "The Problem of the Historical Jesus," **Essays on New Testament Themes** (London: S. C. M. Press, 1965), pp. 144-150; W. Pannenberg, **op. cit.,** pp. 53-66; R. H. Fuller, **op. cit.,** pp. 102-108 and 130. The latter sees Jesus' message and ministry as the proleptic presence of God's kingdom (p. 104).

the blind receive their sight and the lame walk, lepers are cleansed and the deaf hear, and the dead are raised up, and the poor have the good news preached to them."[10] Jesus' words and deeds brought hope and mercy to those who needed it. He was simultaneously God's justice vindicating the oppressed and God's judgment on the oppressor. He initiated the festivities of the eschatological wedding banquet where the outcasts, those wandering the highways and byways, were welcome and were appreciated.[11] Pannenberg believes Jesus was put to death precisely for fraternizing with sinners and outcasts and promising them a share in the kingdom of God. Such activity nullified Jewish law and was considered blasphemous.[12] Jesus was condemned for a way of living in which every person had value before God.

Jesus' message was not a static word but a dynamic way of living. He went out to people and in that way showed them that they were worthwhile. He loved the outcast and the sinner and so restored them. What he really did was give himself to others. Or as Bonhoeffer put it so well—he was a man for others.

As Jesus reflected upon the way of life he had begun, he

---

10. Matt. 11:2-5. R. Fuller insists that in his answer to John, preserved by this passage from Q, Jesus simply interprets his preaching and healings as the beginnings of God's eschatological action as promised in Isaiah 35 and 61. Mark 1:9-13 which interprets the baptism of Jesus according to Isaiah 64:1 and 42:1 is seen as a later christological statement. **Op. cit.,** pp. 116-118 and 128.

11. Cf. Matt. 11:16-19. Compare with Mk. 2:19 (Matt. 9:15 and Lk. 5:34); Mtt. 22:1-14; Mtt. 25:1-13; Jo. 2:1-11; and Mk. 14:25 (Mtt. 26:29; Lk. 22:18). Ernst Fuchs centered upon Jesus' **conduct** as the embodiment of his preaching. When Jesus sat at table with tax collectors and sinners he was announcing that the eschatological banquet, which tradition had expected for the righteous, had already come. By his fraternizing with sinners Jesus revealed God's mercy and for that reason could later be proclaimed Christ by the community: **Das urchristliche Sakramentsver-ständnis** (Bad Cannstatt: R. Müllerschön Verlag, 1958), pp. 37ff.; "The Quest of the Historical Jesus," **Studies of the Historical Jesus** (Naperville, Ill.: Allenson, 1964), pp. 11-31.

12. **Jesus: God and Man,** pp. 251-258. Consider the following texts: John 5:5-18 and 19:7; Mk. 2:15-17 (Mt. 9:10-13, Lk. 5:29-32); Mt. 11:16-19 (Lk. 7:29-35); Lk. 7:36-50; Lk. 19:1-10; John 8:1-11 and 9:1-41.

probably came to appreciate that it was a road filled with risks.[13]
Going out to others involves a dropping of one's defenses. To share
sorrows, to touch lepers, to laugh at a wedding requires that one
not wear a coat of armor. To show concern and to wash the feet
of one's followers is to make oneself vulnerable. Others may take
advantage. They may resent one's approach especially if they
are not strong enough to imitate it or fear a loss of prestige and
adulation for themselves. Vested interests and feelings of inadequacy before a sincere and gifted person sometimes turn into
destructive forces.

As Jesus grew in his consciousness of himself and his mission
he would have experienced uncertainty about the reaction of
others, the problems caused by being misunderstood or misjudged,
and the haunting fear of failure when some rejected him.[14] The
treatment accorded prophets, including John the Baptist, certainly
raised the premonition of death; yet Jesus felt impelled not to
change his approach.[15] He had to confront others for it was his
mission. What they did to him did not matter. He had to continue
speaking and acting, no matter what the reaction and the consequences.

---

13. Cf. Lk. 13:32-33. Jesus decision to go up to Jerusalem primarily
involved the determination to bring his message and ministry of God's
kingdom to the heart of Judaism. Since this road would probably lead
to serious conflicts with spiritual and temporal rulers Jesus had to reckon
with the possibility of his death. He decided to continue his mission no
matter what the cost. We do not know the exact moment when Jesus'
readiness to accept death turned into certainty. He had to confront others
with his message and would bear the consequences. That is not to say that
he understood the goal of his mission to be death; passion predictions,
such as Mk. 8:31, 9:31 and 10:33-34, were formulated in retrospect by
the Church: Gunther Bornkamm, op. cit., pp. 154-155; also cf. Hans
Conzelmann, "Jesus Christus," in **Die Religion in Geschichte und Gegen-
wart**, III, edited by K. Galling, third edition (Tübingen: J. C. B. Mohr
(Paul Siebeck), 1957ff.), pp. 619-659.

14. Cf. Jo. 6:66-68 and Lk. 22:28.

15. What happened to his cousin, John the Baptist, probably served
as a warning to Jesus. But it did not deter him from bringing the Kingdom
to every person, even to those whose rejection might result in violence
to his person: R. Fuller, **op. cit.**, p. 107; J. Knox, **op. cit.,**, p. 102. According

John Knox rightly contends that Jesus did not purposely intend his death.[16] His death was not a physical fact preordained by the Father. Nor was it something he presented to the Father in satisfaction.[17] The crucifixion was the almost inevitable result of reaching out to others in an attempt to remove their hardness of heart. Jesus was the human extension of God's struggle, of suffering love, on behalf of reconciliation in a world suffering from hostility and disunity.[18] Those who killed Jesus wanted to take away his life so he couldn't give it away any more; they wanted no part of his struggle. They could not understand that God was in Christ reconciling the world to himself (2 Cor. 5:19).

As Schoonenberg notes, the most important aspect of Jesus' *kenosis* was not his humility in moving from divinity to humanity, nor was it the death event. Schoonenberg sees it as a decision taken by the Son made man.[19] It was the total process and style

---

to J. Jeremias (Zimmerli-Jeremias, **The Servant,** p. 102) martyrdom was then considered part of the prophetic vocation. Eduard Lohse raises the question how Jesus might have interpreted the possibility of his death if he did not see himself as the suffering servant of Isaiah 53. According to Lohse the idea of vicarious atonement by death was present in Palestinian Judaism. That later became the foundation for applying Isaiah 53 to Jesus: **Märtyrer und Gottesknecht: Untersuchungen zur urchristlichen Verkundigung vom Sührttod Jesu Christi—Forschungen zur Religion und Literatur des Alten und Neuen Testaments,** 64 (Göttingen: Vandenhoeck & Ruprecht, 1955), pp. 64-110.

16. **Op. cit.,** pp. 62-63. We have attempted to distinguish Knox's insights regarding Jesus' attitude toward death from his contention that Jesus' true humanity excluded the possibility that he was conscious of being "Son of Man": cf. pp. 58 and 70-73.

17. Cf. Pannenberg, **op. cit.,** p. 277.

18. Cf. Donald M. Baillie, **God Was In Christ: An Essay on Incarnation and Atonement,** second edition (London: Faber and Faber, 1960), pp. 184-202; Daniel Day Williams, **The Spirit and the Forms of Love** (New York: Harper & Row, 1968), p. 185.

19. Piet Schoonenberg, "He Emptied Himself"—Philippians 2, 7 in **Who is Jesus of Nazareth?,** Volume 11 of **Concilium,** edited by E. Schillebeeckx and B. Willems (New York: Paulist Press, 1966), pp. 47-66. On page 55 Schoonenberg says that he begins from Christ's life on earth and not from his preexistence since there never was any other starting point, even for the writers of the New Testament. John Knox notes that Jesus was

of his life that led Jesus to the Father and with him a reconciled humanity. His obedience consisted in his certainty of God's nearness. That confidence, according to Ebeling is the source of faith which opened Jesus to the future.[20] What Jesus brought with him through death was more important than the physical event. The manner and cruelty of his death by crucifixion flowed from the circumstances of time and culture.[21] Its significance came from the meaning he had already created for it—his death was the culmination of his opening himself to others and the future. His goal was to reconcile humanity with the Father and with one another, no matter what their reaction or the consequences for him. Jesus' life and death coupled with the resurrection event was the dynamic revelation that it is safe to love.[22]

Discipleship involves putting on the ways of Jesus, his behavior.[23] One is saved by the personal acceptance and persevering implementation of that message which was Jesus' very life and consciousness: even if others try to prevent one's love and service it will ultimately triumph. But one must take the chance of being hurt in the process of expressing love by word and act, signs and gestures. One cannot go it alone. If love is not to remain isolated and fragmented we need a confidence that the effort is worth it; that it will work out all right. In order that occasional acts of love might become a way of life, there is the need for an openness to the future. If God is more interested in our becoming

---

first regarded simply and naturally as a man, an extraordinary one perhaps, but a man: **The Humanity and Divinity of Christ: A Study of Patterns in Christology** (Cambridge: University Press, 1967), pp. 75-76. This is the reaction to Jesus which Mary Magdalen expresses in **Jesus Christ Superstar**. Reflection and Christology came later. Gustav Aulen provides some interesting insights: **The Drama and the Symbols**, pp. 152-153.

20. Gerhard Ebeling, "Jesus and Faith," in **Word and Faith** (Philadelphia: Fortress Press, 1963), pp. 238-241.

21. J. Knox, **The Death of Christ**, p. 62.

22. Cf. Henri J. M. Nouwen, **Intimacy** (Notre Dame, Ind.: Fides, 1969), p. 36.

23. Cf. Gerhard Ebeling, **The Nature of Faith** (Philadelphia: Fortress Press, 1967—orig. 1961), pp. 46-57.

than in what we are, our openness to the future is an openness to Him and is rightly called faith. Faith is the consciousness that it is safe to love; salvation is the lived implementation of that consciousness.

The *kenosis* of Jesus might also be seen as his conscious rejection of *power*. His significance did not depend upon his claims to be the Son of God, or Lord. According to certain schools of scriptural interpretation Jesus himself made few or no such claims.[24] His significance came from those who were confronted by his word and deed: the powerless blind, lame, lepers, poor, sinners, and outcasts such as publicans and Samaritans. He called for service and not jurisdiction. The "form of a servant" was not a role that Jesus played but the very nature he assumed.[25] Paradoxically he was surrounded by conflict. The reason is that his servanthood was not one of captivity and slavery to destructive powers. He freed persons to be open to God and one another, to life and the future. The most powerless hour of his life, when he too literally became an outcast, was, according to John, the hour of glory.[26] Even at the moment when the conflict in his life culminated in violence to his person, Jesus refused to hate those who took away his life. Any hope that they might learn to love

---

24. Cf. Wolfhart Pannenberg, **op. cit.**, pp. 53-66, 324-334 and 366; R. Fuller, **op. cit.**, pp. 102-131. No title adequately served to authenticate Jesus' mission. ". . . the secret of his being could only reveal itself to his disciples in his resurrection." So we read in G. Bornkamm: **Jesus of Nazareth**, p. 178. J. Reumann (**op. cit.**, pp. 251-295) has an excellent treatment of the claims of Jesus. Karl Rahner speaks of the self-awareness of Jesus as an unobjectified knowledge: "Dogmatic Reflections on the Knowledge and Self-Consciousness of Christ," in **Theological Investigations**, Volume 5: **Later Writings** (Baltimore: Helicon, 1966), pp. 193-215.

25. Cf. Gunther Bornkamm, "On Understanding the Christ-Hymn: Philippians 2.6-11," in **Early Christian Experience** (New York: Harper & Row, 1969), pp. 115-116.

26. Cf. Jo. 17:1, 4-5. John speaks of a "glory" during the lifetime of Jesus that could be seen only with the eyes of faith. The first sign by which Jesus manifested his glory was at a wedding feast in Cana. (Jo. 2:11) As Jesus dwelt among us we beheld his glory (Jo. 1:14). His last act before the greatest glory of the cross was to wash the feet of his own followers (Jo. 13:1-32).

would be lost if even the one whom they rejected hated in return. In that way the Cross was a symbol of sacramental love; it received its meaning from the way Jesus lived and it effected what it symbolized.[27]

We have resituated Jesus' *kenosis* within his humanity and have identified it as his conscious choice of a certain way of living. It was a divine way of being man. During his public ministry Jesus' life was as varied as ours might be: he experienced misunderstanding, sadness, joy, acceptance by some, and rejection by others.[28] His death was the humanly inevitable climax of a drama lived in positive reaction to the destructive forces of disunity, selfishness, and self-concern. It came to be seen as a promise of new life and peace in the midst of conflict. Jesus' death took its meaning from his way of living. It was the ultimate expression of his openness and vulnerability before others, his acceptance of daily uncertainty from an overriding confidence in the future, his efforts to transform others not by controlling them or imposing himself on them but by continuing to love them and by showing concern. His kingdom was not established by coercion or power but by invitation, by the word which sought to convince.[29] His

---

27. In his approach to the death of Jesus, John Knox sees the cross acting as the symbol of the whole meaning of the whole event of Jesus. "Deliberately he (Knox) chooses the language-terms 'conceptions,' 'images,' 'dramas' rather than the traditional 'theories,' 'explanations,' or even 'historical causes': F. W. Dillistone, "The Atonement," in Christian History and Interpretation: Studies Presented to John Knox, edited by W. R. Farmer, C. F. D. Moule, and R. R. Niebuhr (Cambridge: University Press, 1967), p. 53.

28. Matthew 11:19 indicates that Jesus was branded a glutton and a drunkard for eating and drinking with tax collectors and sinners. John 6:66-67 pictures Jesus as feeling the pain of rejection.

29. Pannenberg notes that Jesus directly granted eschatological salvation: "That is, the nearness of the Kingdom of God that he proclaimed is itself salvation for those who take notice of it." He then continues: "The nearness of the Kingdom of God signifies a threat of judgment only for those who close themselves to it by seeking to fulfill their lives in striving for riches, in their own righteousness, and in care for their own well-being. The others who direct their vision beyond their own accomplishments and possessions toward God's future have salvation already in

kingdom freed persons from the routine of ritual and raised an appreciation of the value of life itself beyond any concern with possessions, status, or the proscriptions against sinners and out-casts.[30] To appreciate the earth, the sun, the sky, people, and animals, without simply trying to own them or control them is a point of departure that is alive, free, and spontaneous.[31] To continue such a life even when it causes others to be threatened and threaten is the hope that Jesus proved possible.

Early Christianity attempted to continue Jesus' *Way* of living by its stress on the ideals of experienced fellowship (*koinonia*), eucharist, and shared hospitality.[32] It realized that worry about one's own bread was material, but worry about the bread of an-other was spiritual. It had Jesus' insight that if all of us were truly concerned about one another's bread and clothing, no one would be hungry or naked, and no one would have to worry about himself or herself. Discipleship in its most positive expression was

---

this attitude. Therefore those are especially to be called blessed who in their situation have no other hope than God's future: ... (Luke 6:20f.). Because salvation, the fulfilled destiny of man, consists in the fulfillment of openness for God, it is already present for those who long for the near-ness of God proclaimed by Jesus; it has already come to those who hear and accept Jesus' message of the imminent Kingdom of God. Jesus does not decide whether such hearing and accepting happens in an individual case, but declares it to be a matter for the coming judgment ... (cf. Mtt. 13:24-30 and 47-50). Because the future salvation was already present in Jesus' preaching, he did not preach in the desert as the Baptist did, but went to men in their cities and where they lived." **Jesus-God and Man,** pp. 227-228. Christian Duquoc finds it significant that Jesus always refused to prove himself or to impose himself on man. He would not resort to power even before Pilate: "The Hope of Jesus" in **Dimensions of Spirituality,** edited by Duquoc (New York: Herder & Herder, 1970), pp. 21-30.

---

30. Cf. Mk. 2:23-28 (Mt. 12:1-8, Lk. 6:1-5); Mk. 3:1-6 (Mt. 12:9-14, Lk. 6:6-11); Mk. 7:1-23 (Mt. 15:1-20); Lk. 11:37-54; Lk. 14:1-6; Mt. 6:25-34 (Lk. 12:22-31). Cf. also note 12.

31. The concept of Jesus' trust in living is central to Leander E. Keck: **A Future for the Historical Jesus** (Nashville and New York: Abingdon, 1971). Francis of Assisi's original rule of love intended such a life: cf. Paul Sabatier, **The Life of Francis of Assisi** (New York: Scribners, 1930), p. 253.

32. Cf. Acts 2:42-46 and 4:32-35.

an openness to life itself which transcended even elemental economic self-concern. Faith involved putting on the attitudes and consciousness of Jesus. Such a giving of self in the here and now situations of life has been termed a radical obedience. Perhaps it is better called an openness to life as surprise or consciously chosen vulnerability.

Although the persecutions and their Christian martyrs did much to enhance the growth of early Christianity, I sometimes think they were at the same time responsible for an individualistic and morbid spirituality. The ideal Christian became more the martyr who imitated Jesus by suffering physical torment and death, rather than the person who imitated the life of Jesus by being willing to take a risk in his relationships with other people, simply because they were people and should therefore be his brothers and sisters. I believe that Polycarp's stress on interior attitudes affirming life is preferable to Ignatius of Antioch's search for material martyrdom.[33] To consciously and willingly accept the possibility of being wounded or hurt by others, to admit error and failure, to change, to acknowledge the need for continuous development, to express sadness and joy, to wish others well, to trust God and neighbor, to show kindness, to need others to love are really more important than to physically die. Every death, even that of martyrdom, really has value only from the life a person brings through it.

To be a disciple of Jesus does not mean running away from life but confronting it without anxiety and fear. Discipleship's best expression need not be martyrdom or even the monastic life which later substituted the former's physical death with its spiritual death. It may be good to state bluntly that the troubles of institutionalized religious orders in our times may be a good sign. The Spirit may be reminding us that what Jesus had to say and do he worked out in everyday existence. He did not become an Essene. It was his attempt to live freely, and not conformity

---

33. Compare Ignatius, **Epistle to the Romans** 4-7 with Polycarp, **Epistle to the Philippians** 3 and 8:2.

to some pattern imposed by the Father, that brought his untimely death. He didn't want the death. He was determined to continue living in a full sense, to create an environment conducive to living, and to invite others to share the wonder and discovery that the experiment of life is. God's kingdom which was proleptically present in his activity was lifegiving. Jesus' refusal to stop living and teaching others to live brought him death. And death for life is not really death. That is what the resurrection is all about.

The cross has meaning only in conjunction with the lively life that preceded and followed it. It is a sign of vulnerability for life. To live as a Christian involves an inner commitment to affirm life and its demands. It involves the acceptance of conflict, not on one's own behalf but on behalf of others, that they might live in the fullest sense.[34] Religious life as a Christian does not simply involve accepting life as if it were some pattern which befalls us. It involves a search, creative dissatisfaction with that which is, and a prophetic call for that which should be. To follow Jesus is to be in that way a force for change. But to act at all, to do anything, one must be willing to take a risk. Success is not guaranteed. Whether one's approach is correct, whether one will be accepted, whether one will succeed presupposes the vulnerability which is the willingness to try life and see how it works out. Vulnerability is not simply the acceptance of finitude—it is a basic openness to change and to surprise at where one's openness takes one.

At the same time it is important that we not stereotype vulnerability. Persons grow in their consciousness and develop even as Jesus did. The discovery of life's full meaning and the appreciation of openness and love as values do not come in the same way nor at the same time for every individual. There is the need for time to grow and sometimes to wait for a more opportune moment, or until one is ready for further development and change in a new situation. Such a growth in attitude cannot be implanted by a moral system flowing from a failsafe casuistry. Vulnerability in-

---

34. Cf. J. Metz, **Theology of the World,** pp. 138-139.

volves not a minimalism but a maximalism that flows not simply from training but from the concrete experience of fellowship and *supportive solidarity,* which is what an *Ekklesia* should be. Within the *Ekklesia* Christian leadership is not imposition of a behavioral pattern flowing from jurisdiction and control but the concern and service which seeks to nurture freedom, responsible decision, and openness to others.

Furthermore, the developmental dimension of vulnerability which we propose is not to be confused with an optimistic evolutionism. Jesus did not magically obliterate evil or restore humanity's potential for some unlimited technological perfection. Rather he invites men of every time and culture to continue his struggle of affirming life in its most radical potential. Every person must face the decision whether this world is an opportunity for concern and service to others or an arena for exercising power and control over others. Christian discipleship embodies supportive solidarity with the powerless rather than exploitation. For technological persons the decision whether to align oneself with creative or destructive forces can be more acute than ever, since the survival of humanity depends upon the decision. Perhaps consciously chosen vulnerability in our relationships with one another will ultimately save us more than any dependence upon power. Such an insight has a transcultural value and facilitates the transcultural communication so necessary in our times. Mahatma Gandhi implemented the insight of giving oneself to the world. In becoming powerless he became most effective through Satyagraha, the force of truth and love. He wrote "Satyagraha is the vindication of truth not by infliction of suffering on the opponent but on one's self." The opponent is to be "weaned from error by patience and suffering."[35] His purpose was not to commend suffering to others but to undergo it himself if necessary to effect change. He was by no means proposing an opiate for enduring one's lot. In fact he was reacting against such exploitation as vehemently as Karl

---

35. Louis Fischer, **Gandhi—His Life and Message for the World** (New York: New American Library—Mentor Book, 1954), p. 35.

Marx. Satyagraha had to do with ordinary everyday life and not with any religious elite. Erik Erikson found that fact to be signifi-cant:

> "But for the future it is important to affirm unequivocally that what you call Satyagraha must not remain restricted to ascetic men and women who believe that they can overcome violence only by sexual self disarmament. For the danger of a riotous return of violence always remains at least latent if we do not succeed in imbuing essential daily experience with a Satyagraha-of-everyday life. It is in daily life and especially in the life of children that the human propensity for violence is founded; and we now suspect that much of that excess of violence which distinguishes man from animals is created in him by those child-training methods which set one part of him against another."[36]

In recent years Catholic theology has widened its focus and restored the original unity of the Paschal event, both crucifixion and resurrection. We advocate a more radical extension of horizons which will restore emphasis to the lifestyle of the human Jesus: His giving of self to others which involved an openness to be-coming something new himself.[37] It is this reconciling struggle of Jesus, who was God's struggle incarnate, rather than his suffering on the cross, which Christians should primarily commend to others as a working concept for life. For only within the context of Jesus'

---

36. Erik H. Erikson, **Gandhi's Truth: On the Origins of Militant Non-violence** (New York: W. W. Norton, 1969), p. 234.

37. Our position differs somewhat from that of F. X. Durwell. He says: "In itself the kenosis did not lead Christ towards life in God, for carnal existence stood for sin as against God, and so went counter to that life. Birth according to the flesh placed man at a distance from God, and death, which was the consummation of life according to the flesh, did nothing to lessen that distance. However, in Christ, his freely willed submission to the weaknesses of the flesh, even to their consecration in death, represented the most intense effort to come to God, for it was a submission of obedience, dragging man away from the autonomy of his flesh, and carrying him towards God in a renunciation of self which became, in death, a total renunciation. The kenosis, while being an acceptance of the flesh, was at the same time a complete negation of it." **The Resurrection** (New York: Sheed and Ward, 1960), p. 55. The context in which Durwell interprets the crucifixion is that of a sacrifice in which Jesus freely gives himself as a victim (pp. 59-77).

struggle to live in true openness, with his Father and humanity, is the crucifixion itself a victory rather than a failure. His death was the ultimate decision to remain vulnerable and the final repudiation of power. Such a rejection of control was not a rejection of responsibility nor a passive escape from freedom. It was the culmination of an active, conscious decision to confront others and to remain open to them no matter what the cost and come what may.

I find the concept of vulnerability can be a workable framework for interpreting the message which was Jesus' life. It might sensitize Christians to the need for change, responsible development, and communal confrontation, rather than allow mere dues paying conformity and security. It offers a dynamic alternative to an overly individualistic spirituality whose language centered on passive resignation and obedience. The vulnerability of Jesus flowed from his word and action. Many Christians, buffeted by the insecurities, anxieties, limitations, and injustices of life, have misinterpreted the imitation of Christ into a protective escape from freedom. The struggle that was Jesus' life, and is his life, has too often faded into some passive form upon the cross.

Salvation interpreted as consciously chosen vulnerability or the decision to become affected by those around us involves putting on Jesus' lifestyle and mode of relationship rather than any static increase of reified grace.[38] It is the decision to affirm life in its surprising potential. Such vulnerability which eschews power and control, but not conflict, was the fundamental message which Jesus lived, and from it flows humanization of self and others. By it we live as Jesus did, with unlimited openness to the future from the confidence that God is there.

---

38. Cf. Boniface A. Willems, **The Reality of Redemption** (New York: Herder & Herder, 1970), pp. 24-32.

2 Some Problems in Modern Christology

GERARD S. SLOYAN

It cannot be an easy matter to teach Christology in a systematic way to contemporary undergraduates. There are a number of reasons why I suppose this is so. It is a supposition since I last taught non-biblical theology in 1955. At the undergraduate level I teach the various Christologies of the New Testament to students one third of whom, usually, are Jewish. In two successive New Testament courses we explore the adoptionist Christology of the baptism and transfiguration accounts (with the additional component of Jesus' being made "Lord and Messiah" by his exaltation, Acts 2, 32-36); the "heavenly man" Christology of Mark, which he modifies by stressing that the Son of God must suffer as a man; the Spirit's initiative in bringing Jesus to birth in the infancy narratives of Matthew and Luke; the various levels of Christology in Paul; Christ's preexistence as "word" in John's prologue, as "image" and "firstborn" in the cosmic hymns of Philippians and Colossians, "reflection" and "representation" in Hebrews 1, 3; and finally the divine-human synthesis of Hebrews with its soteriological emphasis on Christ as high priest. In a good year, with a good class, we reach the Christology of Revelation.

The categories Palestinian-Jewish, Jewish-Hellenistic, and Hellenistic are of help here. So is an analysis of the various New Testament titles of Jesus. By the end of a year or even a semester one has the feeling that the Nicaean affirmation that Jesus Christ is "true God of true God," despite its lack of biblical nuance, has begun to make some sense to Jewish ears, and the biblical proposition, "was tempted in every way that we are, yet never sinned" (Heb 4, 15) has come to be accepted for the first time by Christian students.

A difficulty, of course, is that the professor of New Testament studies tends to become impatient with all post-biblical developments and to transmit this impatience to his or her students. Such a stance can easily disqualify one as the expositor of a living, developing religious tradition. It can even make a person the protagonist of a kind of archaism which has as its single principle, "Earlier is better," or, "The Hellenic debased the purity of the Hebraic in Christianity."

Student appreciation of the developed character of belief in Jesus as Christ and Lord has been helpful to us all. There are insoluble questions, of course, like the exact nature of the impact made by the Risen One on the chosen witnesses, or the happenings of the "tunnel period"—A.D. 30 to 50—out of which documents like 1 Thessalonians and the Marcan source if there was one, Q, and "special-Luke" emerged. Nonetheless, there are satisfactions, including that of examining without sophistication the portrait of Jesus that all four gospels in their present, redacted form give us. The initiative to do the latter is usually taken by students. As teachers we may find this portrait teeming with theological, polemic, and apologetic motifs. Students, especially if they are seekers, find in it the path to faith which this conscious preaching of the Church has always provided.

If it is a characteristic shortcoming of biblicists that they do not trouble to keep abreast of the history, politics, and philosophy that overtook the faith of the biblical period and helped to erect a post-biblical theological edifice, it is equally a flaw of systematic theologians that they are ill at ease with the results of exegesis, which in brief may be defined as exploring *"the text which lies before us* in its present form and in its present context."[1] And just at a time that a generation of systematic theologians attuned to the biblical literature seems to be coming into being, systematics promises to turn into the philosophy of religion.

---

1. Willi Marxsen, tr. Paul J. Achtemeier, **The Beginnings of Christology: A Study of Its Problems**, Facet Books, Biblical Series— 22 (Philadelphia: Fortress, 1969), p. 2.

At the same time, a generation of undergraduate students has appeared which is seemingly disinterested in the entire theological venture, whether marked by a synthesis of its two main components Scripture and philosophy or not. For them, God may be living but theology as an enterprise that compels their interest is dead.

There are several existential situations in the student world which it is important for us to estimate correctly. One is the much spoken of widespread interest in Jesus and disinterest—one may even say correlative disinterest—in the Church or any religious establishment. Another is the unconcern or active hostility toward Christ in those brought up as Christians. (These need not be students; some are colleagues.) The Jesus Christ once central to their faith and piety does not now figure in it or is being systematically replaced by the Buddha, by Gandhi, or by a religious tradition that has no special interest in persons outside the self. Another existential situation is the fellow-feeling many students experience with Jesus as a companion in human weakness so long as no attention is paid to his transcendence, even his human transcendence. Still another is the practical Monophysite character of much parish preaching and of the types of fundamentalist Christianity to which many in the culture are being drawn.

Each of the above situations is influential in its way on what things are possible in a theological exposition of Jesus as the Christ. Some have simply closed their ears to any such exposition. Others will listen up to the point where they discover that their presuppositions are not being shared. A few remain who are interested in exploring who Jesus is as the Christ. These will walk the laborious path of examining what the world of faith or religious concern bases itself upon in believing in him. This is not, of course, evidence in the proper sense but in an analogous one, whereas an exploration of the successive stages of Christology is the object of historical inquiry.

One major temptation of the modern professor is to cleave to a functional Christology while setting an ontological or an ontic one entirely aside. It is undoubtedly of primary importance to know who Jesus was and is *for us*—he who died and rose *propter nostram salutem*. Nonetheless, the thoughtful person cannot sustain this interest for long without wanting to know who Jesus is with respect to God and in himself that he can do this for us. A discovery by the Catholic of the primacy of soteriology over Christology, whether through Paul or Luther, Barth or Bultmann, may account for an enthusiasm as to how salvation works. An unhistorical, metaphysical approach to the person-and-natures question in one's early training may have dulled any appetite for further inquiry. This is especially true if one has had drummed into him an Anselmian formula which attributes infinite worth to every action of a human nature joined to the person of the Word.

Still, the total absence of metaphysics is not a good replacement for bad metaphysics. There should be put in its place a metaphysics that is both true to itself and faithful to the biblical data from which all such speculation arises. All Christology is ultimately soteriological in purpose but one cannot have a building without a first floor. There can be no satisfactory accounting for what Jesus Christ accomplishes if the question of who he is is declared of no consequence or is consistently deferred. That is to say that philosophical speculation can be put aside in the academic inquiry into the religion of the West only at one's peril.

The Christians of the second and third centuries used extra-biblical categories to teach their faith, not because they had lost confidence in the Bible but because they wished to capitalize on the religious and philosophical convictions of those who had never reposed their trust in the biblical books.[2] Hence, men like Justin used the concept "Logos" to describe the way in which God had kept in touch with his world through the philosophers and in Old Testament theophanies before the Logos was uttered in its fullness as Jesus Christ. Later, "Logos" and "Son" fell

---

2. Cf. J. N. D. Kelly, **Early Christian Doctrines** (2nd ed.; London: Adam and Charles Black, 1960), pp. 29-79; Hans Lietzmann, **A History of the Early Church,** I (London: Lutterworth, 1961), 105-23; 173-88.

out of use as terms to describe what God had done in relation to his world, coming to be used exclusively of someone in an eternal relation with the Father. A complicating factor was the "speculations proceeding from God's eternity (the Father is eternally Father and must thus eternally have a Son) or . . . Origen's Platonic tendency to consider all the spiritual (not merely the Logos but also . . . souls) as pre-existent with regard to the material world and its history."[3] As a result of this tendency, Nicaea in 325 would describe the Son as "of one substance with the Father" (*homoousion tō patri*) before it spoke of his becoming flesh. It meant to affirm against Arius that what is said of God must be said of the Son, though its order in the creed of Nicaea implies, without saying it, that there is an eternal Son of the same substance as the Father who takes flesh. The First Council of Constantinople in 381 likewise referred to begetting from the Father as something which happens "before all ages" (*ton ek tou patros gennēthenta pro pantōn tōn aiōnōn*).

Such terminology flowed from the philosophical assumptions of the times. The New Testament never mentions Jesus' sonship as eternal in the philosophical sense. The Logos, it is true, was "with God at the beginning" (Jn 1, 2). Further, he who is called God's "dear Son . . . exists before everything, and all things are held together in him" (Col 1, 13. 17). The Christological hymn in which the latter phrase appears (1, 15-20) puts Christ in the place of God's image, wisdom, and word as understood by Hellenistic Judaism, wisdom being the pre-existent agent of creation which was with God from the beginning.[4] There is also the possibility that this concept had fused with that of a

---

3. Piet Schoonenberg, **The Christ** (New York: Herder and Herder, 1971), p. 81.

4. Cf. Eduard Lohse, **Colossians and Philemon**, in "Hermeneia—A Critical and Historical Commentary on the Bible" (Philadelphia: Fortress, 1971), pp. 46-61; C. F. D. Moule, **The Epistles of Paul the Apostle to the Colossians and to Philemon** (Cambridge: At the University Press, 1968), pp. 58-71; Jack T. Sanders, **The New Testament Christological Hymns** (ibid., 1971), pp. 75-87.

cosmic redeemer in pre-Christian Judaism, but this is hypothetical. Clearly, however, Christ is being described as preexistent in the manner of divine wisdom.

Colossians will also speak of the secret hidden for long ages (v. 26; cf. 2, 2), as "Christ in you, the hope of a glory to come" (1, 27). Hence, God's long-standing counsel about what he meant to do for us culminates in the revelation (v. 26) made in Christ. The Son "is before all else that is (*pro pantōn*)"; in him, everything "continues in being" (*synestēken*), a verb favored by Platonic and Stoic philosophy. This emphasizes Christ's unique position as Lord over the cosmos. Similar belief in Christ's pre-existence is voiced by the hymns of Phil 2, 6-11; 1 Tim 3, 16; Pet 3, 18-19. 22; Jn 1, 1-5. 9-11. All seem to stem from a common mythical conception. The question raised by these hymns is, Does God eternally have with him a Christ, a Son, who became a redeemer in time, or does he eternally have within himself his wisdom, revealed as the Christ? From eternity does he have the intention of bringing to birth a human Son, a perfect embodiment of himself, through whom all things in heaven and on earth will be reconciled, or does he have an eternal Son who comes to be thus embodied?

Man cannot know how it is with God in eternity. Just as obviously, there can be no statement of Scripture to enlighten him on the point, no matter how much that appearance may be given. There can only be an affirmation in Scripture that the hidden God has bodied forth an image of himself in time, an image which of necessity was always with him, like all that is himself. This conception had an existence in Hellenist Gentile and possibly in Hellenist Jewish circles. Jesus dead, risen, and in glory fulfilled the terms of this conception admirably. He was therefore inserted into it as the preexistent image of God made visible in time.

Whether a full-blown redeemer myth existed or not, the Hebrew Bible in its later books and the post-biblical Jewish literature spoke freely of God's wisdom and his word as being with him as if from everlasting (*me'olam,* Prv 8, 23; cf. Wis Sol 7, 25f.; Sir 1, 1. 4.).The New Testament spoke of his *logos, eikōn, charaktēr,* as being with him in the same way. Whatever is properly "of God" is by definition eternal. Any manifestation of the divine, any knowledge we have of the divine which flows from such manifestation, is by definition temporal. When the New Testament uses Stoic vocabulary it inclines toward the familiar changelessness of God found in that thought system as contrasted with the mobility and contingency of the world (cf. Col 1, 15; Heb. 1, 3). This occasional New Tesament usage becomes the consistent assumption of a second and third-century Church trying to convey biblical concepts.

The New Testament leaves in no doubt whatever that God, who is one, is the object of the prayer and devotion of the man Jesus in his earthly days. Jesus is never portrayed in terms of duality, least of all as if he were in dialogue with any divine Logos or Spirit dwelling within him. He is totally open to God. He is never reported as having anything in common with human sinfulness. He spends himself utterly, out of a conscious conviction of his vocation to bring about in his hearers readiness for the last age.[5] The Jesus of the New Testament undergoes real change after his death. In his risen life, which is anything but a resuscitation and resumption of his former life (the phrases "died" and "was buried," 1 Cor 15, 3f., ensure this), he is recognized by believers as the One through whom God will save. His life had been one of total self-giving, of accepting sinners in table-fellowship, of doing his Father's will wherever it led him. Now he is viewed as exalted by God for this obedience as the Lord of the final age, as the visible manifestation of that eternal self-giving which is God himself.

The Christology of the New Testament distinguishes sharply between Jesus crucified and Christ risen, a distinction all but erased two centuries later by a preaching of him which conceived him as the same at all points of his earthly and risen life since he was God's Son, indeed, his eternal Son. (Recall that only in

---

5. Cf. Eduard Schweizer, tr. David E. Green, **Jesus** (Richmond: John Knox, 1971), esp. pp. 123-68.

the Christological hymn of Col 1, 15-20, is the "image" and "firstborn" in, through, and unto whom everything was created identified with "the Son of his love." The hymn is inserted after mention of the Son who has acted as the redeemer of man in time). This contravention of the biblical record was not thought to be such by its earnest Greek partisans. It was a necessary mode of thought in men for whom the spiritual and the divine was real, the corporal and the human unreal or less real. In the New Testament, God's raising up of Jesus in glory made all the difference in the latter's power to save. In second and third-century thought, the fact of eternal divine Sonship, identified with status as the Logos, made that difference.[6]

Early struggles with gnostic thought resulted in the docetist dualism about Christ that we are apprised of in the reports of Hegesippus and Irenaeus, which Eusebius later transmits.[7] These tendencies emerged in their orthodox form as a *Logos-sarx* Christology, the distinctive orthodox feature of which was that the sarx is a real and not an apparent humanity.[8] An important exchange took place some sixty years before the Arian crisis when Dionysius, bishop of Alexandria (247/8—64/5), received a letter from Dionysius, bishop of Rome, on the subject of Christology.[9] Writing in 262, the Roman Dionysius took a stand against both Sabellian modalists and tritheists. He addressed himself to the Alexandrian bishop because a previous synod in Rome had condemned certain propositions attributed to him on the basis of criticisms of the bishops of Cyrenaica.[10] The latter, Sabellian in tendency, had accused Dionysius of Alexandria,

---

6. "Preoccupied with the Logos, they [the Apologists, Justin apart] evince surprisingly little interest in the Gospel Figure.... For Melito.... His pre-existence and complete identification with the Godhead were strongly stressed." Kelly, **Early Christian Doctrines**, p. 145.

7. Eusebius, **Hist. Eccl.** 3, 26ff.; 4, 7f.; 4, 22.

8. Cf. Kelly, pp. 153-58.

9. Denzinger-Schönmetzer, **Enchiridion Symbolorum** (32 ed.; Barcelona: Herder, 1963), sec. 112-15.

10. Athanasius, **Epistola de sententia Dionysii episcopi Alexandrini,** 5, **PG** 15, 1103ff.; cf. Eusebius, **HE** 7, 6, 26.

a pupil of Origen, of separating and estranging the Son from the Father; of asserting that the Son did not exist before being engendered (which would mean that he was not eternal); and of viewing the Son as a creation (*poiēma*) and a product (*genēton*), someone foreign to the Father as the vine is to the vine-dresser or the ship to the shipwright. Finally, he was accused of saying that Christ is not consubstantial (*homoousios*) with God.[11]

Dionysius of Alexander had taken a stand against Sabellius who, his doctrine having been condemned by Pope Callistus in 217, returned from Rome to his native Cyrenaica, then died (before 257). We do not have Sabellius' own witness, only the charge that he took the monarchian tendency of Epigonus, which Popes Zephyrinus and Callistus had favored, to an extreme. In Sabellius' hands the teaching was said to have so stressed the divine unity that proper divine substance was denied to the Son. His opponents were prone to say that he confused the Father and the Son.[12] When the learned Dionysius of Alexandria wrote a memorandum refuting Sabellius it fell into Roman hands. There, because the monarchian spirit was strong, it netted the admonition of Pope Dionysius. The Roman bishop reprobated the teaching which held, in some fashion (*tropon tina*), he said, for three gods, dividing the "holy unity (*hagian monada*) into three different *hypostaseis* entirely separated (*kechōrismenas*) from each other."[13] "For it is necessary for the divine Logos to be united (*henōsthai*) to the God of all and for the Holy Spirit to remain and dwell (*emphilochōrein . . . kai endiaitasthai*) in God."[14] This plea for a divine Trinity that could be "capitulated and brought together" (*sygkephalaiousthai te kai synagesthai*) into "a summit, so to say" (*hōsper eis koryphēn tina*) shows the tendency to stress what

---

11. For a summary of the exchange, cf. Jean Daniélou in "The First Six Hundred Years," Vol. I of the **The Christian Centuries** (London: Darton, Longman, and Todd), written with Henri Marrou; pp. 214-17.

12. Cf. Athanasius, **ibid.**

13. DS 112.

14. **Ibid.**

we would call unity of substance as opposed to the Origenist stress on distinctness of persons.

The Roman bishop does not deny the separation of persons but resists it in a form attributed to Nestorius that would end with the distinction made between the Word and Jesus as two personal centers. In later terminology, each would be constituted by its own act of being, though analogously, as in all statements about God and man. The Alexandrian Dionysius sent a spirited response to his Roman brother, *Refutation and Apology,* of which Athanasius in his *Sententia Dionysii* has preserved important parts.

This exchange served as a prelude to the Arian teaching that led to anathematization by the Council of Nicaea. Arius, a priest of Alexandria, in 318 (or possibly in 323) began by teaching the complete substantial equality of the Father and the Logos, then shifted to the originality and privileges of the Father. Only the Father was *agennētos,* i.e., not engendered, not become, one who had not entered into being. He alone is absolute beginning, *archē,* with respect to all other beings. Omitting in too great detail matters already well known, we summarize Arius' teaching (which he traced to Lucian, a priest of Antioch): he subordinated the Logos to God in such a way that his opponents could say that he taught that "There was a when-the-Word-did-not-exist" and that the Word was a perfect "divine" creature not to be compared with other created beings.

Constantine convoked a council to bring peace and impose a single settlement as part of imperial good order. A powerful majority of bishops opposed the Arian view. Despite the conservative objection that *homoousios* was not only non-biblical but had a recent history of conveying the exact opposite notion, namely the "same in personhood" (it had been rejected at a synod at Antioch in 268 as modalist),[15] the creed and canons of Nicaea were promulgated.[16] What they chiefly intended was an affirmation that in Jesus there is a reality that is fully divine, that in him

15. Cf. Daniélou, "The First Six Hundred Years," p. 218.
16. Cf. DS 125, 130.

the "complete being (*pan to plēroma*) of the godhead (*theotētos*) dwells embodied (*somatikōs*)," as Col 2, 9 has it. To ensure this New Testament affirmation, phrases were multiplied such as *Theon ek Theou, phōs ek phōtos, Theon alēthinon ek Theou alēthinou, gennēthenta ou poiēthenta, homoousion tō patri,* all meant to put the matter beyond denial by any verbal wiles of the Arian party. The opinions were anathematized which said that, "The Son of God [originated] from no one, and that there was a [time] when (*pote hote*) he was not, and that because of free will he was capable of good and evil, and that he was to be designated a creature and one brought into being."

The Nicaean creed gives the impression that it requires the *eternal begetting* of the Son. This is because of the supposition that such was the sole alternative to the begetting of a creature-Logos before the world of time. The traditional phrases from the creed of Caesarea on which it was based, "Son of God . . . sole [*monogenē*] . . . God of God . . . Light of Light" did not seem to guarantee Christ's full divinity sufficiently and so "of the same substance with the Father" was added. What the Nicaean formula requires is that Jesus Christ the Son of God be worshipped as true God. It assumes as part of this, without using the term, an eternal begetting as Son. If, as shall be later held in this paper, it cannot be established from the New Testament that this Son existed as Son from eternity (although in fact such may have been the case), but only that at his human begetting he was such a one that he must be called consubstantial with the Father—a matter made manifest at his exaltation—then his begetting of the substance of the Father is something we know of from the time of his human birth. Not only was this birth eternally intended. There was also the creation of all things in, through, and unto him who in time would be known as the Son of God.

This interpretation of Nicaea seems essential, for the maximalist one which makes a philosophical position on the presumed inner nature of God a matter of Christian faith leads to insuperable difficulties. The chief of these is that an eternal divine Son— something nowhere affirmed in Scripture—is, by an inevitable theological process, the hypostasis who becomes the act of being of a human nature. The opposite situation seems to suit the biblical data better on every count: a human hypostasis with its own act of being, a Son of God who begins to be known in time, who must be called divine because his birth was the personal beginning of the human history of God the Logos. This is a Christology of God's total presence in Jesus. The Word is enhypostatic in the man who is the Christ, the son of the living God. His human nature is his own, not anhypostatic, impersonal, supplied for by the person of the Word who is its act of being.

A development that should be noticed is the activity of Apollinaris (c. 310—c. 390) bishop of Laodicaea in Syria, a Nicaean, who wrote (in 363) that in the incarnation "the divine Word plays the role of the vital principle normally played in the ordinary man by the spirit or soul."[17] As he expressed it, "Unique is the physis (concrete reality) of the divine Word which was made incarnate."[18] *Mia physis tou Theou logou sesarkōmenē.* Apollinaris seems to have been echoing, in his view of the one divine-human nature of Christ, Malchion, a priest of Antioch. Malchion led the fathers of a synod (268) in that city in a condemnation of the teaching of Paul of Samosata by saying that Christ's union as God with his human nature was like that which exists between a soul and a body.[19] The Word is in Christ as the soul is in us, as later full-fledged Apollinarism was to teach. In Apollinaris' outlook, the Word was united to a body and not to a human soul. Pope Damasus wrote against this position about 374, saying that if an imperfect man were taken on (*susceptus est*) our salvation would be imperfect, since we needed saving in body and soul[20]—the Son of Man having come to save that which was lost (cf. Mt. 18, 11.) The same pope condemned the Apollinarists

---

17. Henri Marrou in "The First Six Hundred Years," p. 262; cf. J. Daniélou, in **ibid.**, p. 218.

18. Ps-Athanasius (Apollinaris) **Ad Jovianum,** in H. Lietzmann, **Apollinaris von Laodicaea und seine Schule** (1904), p. 251, lines 1-3.

19. Text in H. de Riedmatten, **Les Actes du procès de Paul de Samosate** (1952).

20. DS 146.

in 378, giving the same reason. He wrote: "Anyone who holds Christ to be in any way lacking in deity or humanity shows himself possessed by a diabolic spirit. . . ."[21]

The turbulent half-century of Christological debate after Nicaea, much of it politically conditioned, led to the calling of I Constantinople by Theodosius in 381. This brought a definition of the divinity of the Holy Spirit against the party of Macedonius (*Pneumatomachoi*) and certain other additions to the creed of Constantinople: "maker of *heaven and earth* . . . the *only* Son of God . . . begotten of the Father *before all ages* [in place of "begotten from the substance of the Father"] *took flesh of the Holy Spirit and the Virgin Mary* . . . *was crucified for us under Pontius Pilate* . . . *was buried* . . . *and rose again* . . . *according to the Scriptures* . . . *sits at the right hand of the Father* . . . will come *again in glory* . . . *and of his kingdom there will be no end.*" All of the phrases about the Holy Spirit in the creed said at the Roman Mass are additions of I Constantinople, since at Nicaea it had ended abruptly, "and in the Holy Spirit."

An opponent of Apollinaris, Diodorus of Tarsus, came forward in the 370's as an early member of what came to be called the Antiochean school featuring a "Christology of ascent." His best-known pupil was John Chrysostom but the transmitter of his characteristic teaching was Theodore, bishop of Mopsuestia in Cilicia (392-428), who lived his life in peace but was anathematized posthumously (553) as responsible for the "blasphemies" of his pupil Nestorius. The latter, an Antiochean monk, was made bishop of Constantinople by Theodosius II in 428 and immediately began preaching sermons which pressed the most extreme conclusions of the Antiochean school: that the two natures in Christ were so distinct that we cannot say accurately that the Word suffered in the passion; that Mary should not be called *Theotokos* since she gave birth to a man; and that the Infant Jesus should not be called by the name of God. This healthy corrective to Apollinarism, with its attempt to ensure the full humanity of

---

21. DS 149.

Christ, nonetheless foundered on its total separation of what was man in Christ and what was God. The Catholic response was made at Ephesus with the use of twelve propositions of anathema by Cyril of Alexandria.[22] The Council ran from June to October of 431, when the emperor dismissed it for not having achieved reconciliation between the forces of the two patriarchs, Cyril and Nestorius. It did, however, manage to proclaim the basic unity of the person of Christ: "Although the natures (*physeis*) are different, by coming together in a true union (*pros henotēta tēn alēthinen synenechtheisai*) there results from the two one Christ and Son (*heis de ex amphoin Christos kai Huios*), not as though the differences of natures are removed by (*dia*) the union (*henosin*) but that divinity and humanity by this mysterious and indescribable union (*syndromēs*) are joined in one person (*pros henotēta*), become for us the one Lord Jesus Christ and Son."[23]

Cyril's thought, here expressed in his second letter to the Council which it adopted, is a perfect example of the *Logos-sarx* Christology of Alexandria, while Nestorius' position, expressed in a reply to Cyril condemned by the Council, is equally representative of Antiochean *Logos-anthrōpos* thought. Nestorius did the litigants the Catholic service of preserving Christ's complete manhood but he was unable to establish how the human Christ whom Mary bore was at the same time God. He protested manfully against the Alexandrian tendency to divinize *sarx,* in words such as these: "They say that flesh did not remain flesh after the resurrection but changed over into the nature of the godhead . . . using the very word 'deification'."[24] It was unavailing. The Apollinarist-tending Cyril won the day. A formula of union was worked out in 433 in which both sides gave a little, the party of St. Cyril and, for the Nestorians, of John of Antioch. The formula received the Antiochean contribution while tempering Cyril's tendency to speak of one divine *hypostasis* and *physis* in Christ. It likewise prepared

---

22. DS 252-63.
23. DS 250.
24. Letter to Pope Celestine, PL48, 176f.; E. Schwartz, ed. **Acta Conciliorum Oecumenicorum** (1914), I, 2, 13.

the way for the phrasing of Chalcedon two decades later by saying: "We confess our Lord Jesus Christ . . . perfect God and perfect man . . . consubstantial with the Father in his godhead, consubstantial with us in his manhood. A union has taken place of two natures (*physeis*). And so we confess one Christ, one Son, one Lord."[25]

Alexandrian theology mustered its forces once again in the person of Eutyches, archimandrite of a monastery at Constantinople numbering over three hundred monks. This man, already old in 447-48 but having great support at court, set about consolidating Cyrillian sentiment throughout the East. His tendency was directly opposed to the Nestorian. His enemies charged him with teaching that Jesus Christ was formed "from two natures" (*ek duo physeōn*) and that in the resulting union only one remains— hence, the term "Monophysite." He took literally and to excess the Apollinarist-Cyrillian formula, "Unique (*Mia*) is the nature of the Word incarnate." The learned Roman bishop Leo I intervened when the emperor called a council at Ephesus in 449, urged to do so by Eutyches whose views had been condemned at Constantinople the previous autumn. Leo wrote a letter (*Tomus*) to Flavian, bishop of Constantinople, in which he formulated the Christological problem clearly and precisely. Dioscorus of Alexandria presided in a high-handed manner at the "Robber Synod of Ephesus" in 449, taking a leaf out of Cyril's book by imitating his behavior at the council in the same city some eighteen years before. The papal letter was set aside at this meeting, Eutyches was rehabilitated, and numerous opponents thought to be Nestorians were deposed from their sees. The death of Theodosius II in July, 450, brought a turn in the tide. In autumn of the year following a council was convoked by the imperial successors, Martin and Pulcheria, who were favorable to the pope.

The terms of the Chalcedonian settlement are well known.

---

25. **PG** 77, 176f.; Schwartz **ACO**, I, 1, 4; cf. J. M. Carmody and T. E. Clarke, eds. **Sources of Christian Theology**, Vol. III, "Christ and His Mission" Westminster, Maryland: Newman, 1966), 111.

A creed was agreed upon which derived largely from Leo's *Tome,* though the phrases of the latter were supplemented and elaborated. It confessed, "one single Christ, Son, Lord, Unique (*monogenē*), in two natures (*physesin*), without confusion (*asygchytōs*), without change (*atreptōs*), without division (*adiarētōs*), without separation (*achoristōs*), the difference of natures being in no way suppressed by the union (*henosin*), but rather the properties of each (*tis idiotētos . . . physeōs*) being safeguarded and reunited (*syntrechousēs*) in (*eis*) a single person (*prosōpon*) and a single hypostasis."[26] From this definition the familiar formula *mia hypostasis en duo physesin* has been extracted.

Chalcedon was a masterpiece of balance between the two principal warring factions, the Alexandrian and Antiochean, and their extremes, the Monophysite and Nestorian positions, as each was spelled out by its opponents. It is a commonplace nowadays to say that Chalcedon was a beginning and not an end, a statement of the Christological problem and not a solution; that it brought two opposed Christologies together but did not entirely reconcile them. All this is true but the 5th-century Council should at least be credited with expressing biblical faith in the personal unity of Jesus Christ, of whom it could be said that all that pertained to man pertained to him and all that pertained to God pertained to him. This was no little verbal feat for a Greek-speaking world (with Syriac, Coptic, and Latin in use out at its periphery) that had not had peace on the question in two hundred years.

We have been invited in various ways since the fifteenth centenary observance of 1951 to go beyond Chalcedon in our theology. Serviceable as it may have been as a statement of faith, the theology which underlay it is inadequate for our times—just as all faith statements and all theologies betray their inadequacy with the passage of time. What can be overlooked, or at least understressed, in an invitation such as this, is the variety of theological "orthodoxies" that came along to encrust Chalcedon (coupled with the statements against both Monergists and Mono-

---

26. DS 302.

thelites of III Constantinople in 680-81). These developments, especially the nonconciliar ones, make it hard to go back to the Chalcedonian fork in the road.

We have pointed out that from the creeds that led to Nicaea and onward, culminating in I Constantinople (381), the eternal preexistence of the Son *as Son* was assumed without being argued. Both the Nestorian position and the Catholic one at III Constantinople, the declaration that in Christ there were two principles of operation and two wills, held for a duality not only of natures in Christ but also of sets of activities. The 5th and 6th centuries witnessed a retrenchment that is called "Neo-Chalcedonianism" but in fact was post-Chalcedonian revisionism—something like the current papal promulgation of Vatican II which in certain respects is a negation of it. In effect, Chalcedon's phrases were repeated but Cyril's teaching and the terminology of the twelve anathemas was more and more admitted. The definition of hypostasis given by Leontius of Byzantium, "that which exists by itself" (*to kath'eauto*), was applied to the divine Word. Christ's humanity became, by contrast, that which does not exist by itself. All the Antiochean attempts to remind the Church of what the gospels said about the man Jesus were defeated by a divine hypostasis which overpowered all. The Chalcedonian West lost large elements of membership to the Monophysite East centered in Egypt and Syria. Meanwhile, Monophysitism made progress within Chalcedonian orthodoxy through the teaching of Severus of Antioch, the center of whose piety was the eternal Word. "His unity was exalted above everything else, the two natures being distinguished only by virtue of a logical, not a real distinction."[27]

Chalcedon had no choice in its role of reconciliation but to acknowledge a duality of natures in Christ according to the Antiochean pattern. But of this duality as such the New Testament knows nothing. It tells of a man who has a man's nature and who is so suffused with divinity that he is unique in his stance before

---

27. Marrou, op. cit., p. 362.

God. He is God's Son and ultimately his exalted or glorified Son. For this human life and this exaltation, preparation has been made in eternity by a preexistence of some sort. Jesus Christ is the image and the effulgence of the eternal God. In him and through him and for him, a creaturely world has its existence. He is central to God's plan for the world. But of a duality in his person, a divine-human tension, a consciousness of being in any sense two rather than one, the New Testament says nothing. As to any actions or passions of his that are more fittingly attributed to his divinity or his humanity, any such supposition contradicts the scriptural record entirely. Consequently we must hold that the sole truth being protected in the two-natures formula of Chalcedon is the reality of humanity conjoined uniquely to divinity, the latter being by definition other than humanity, and precisely in the four ways spelled out by Chalcedon ("inconfusedly, unchangedly, unseparatedly, undividedly"). If the distinction of natures in Christ is unscriptural, Chalcedon tried at least to overcome duality by calling the *hypostasis* or *prosōpon* which he is "the same" seven times.

Post-Chalcedonian developments, including the *Henotikon* of Zeno and the condemnation of the three Antiochean-tending chapters at II Constantinople (553), heightened the unity of Christ as a *divine* person. The adjective "divine" was no part of the definition of Chalcedon but it made its Alexandrian way into the discussion at all points. Leontius of Byzantium would say that the human nature of Christ exists *in* the divine *hypostasis* of the Word.[28]

The explanation prevails down to our own day: the enhypostasia of a human nature in the Word and the anhypostasia of Christ's humanity. Only because of this theological supposition could the question be put, Was Jesus in his humanity the natural Son of God or the adopted son? Because of Alexandrian theology, the former answer was being given in Carolingian times: as man,

---

28. **Adv. nestorianos et eutychianos**, I, passim. PG 44, tomus prior, 1101-66.

Christ is also God's own natural Son. Pseudo-Dionysius spoke of an activity of Christ whereby he brings about what is of man in a superhuman way—the core of a theology of human mediatorship divinely validated.[29] Aquinas allowed to Christ's humanity its own act of being secondary to the being of the Word, but earliest scholasticism would not even call it a "something." Abelard's "Christological nihilism" was responded to with the short-lived theory of an "assumed man." More characteristic of late scholasticism was the position—familiar to many of us—that since essence and act of being are distinct, Christ's humanity does not have its own act of being but exists through the divine act of being of the Word (the theory of Capreolus and Billot). This is the end of the line, in a sense, of speculation on the faith-statements of Chalcedon: a human nature of Christ that is completely unreal and far separated from the New Testament picture of him.

Let us proceed as briefly as we can to a Catholic Christology that is faithful to the New Testament data and the Councils, both of them correctly viewed with respect to what they wished to affirm and the ways in which they were limited by the understandings of their times.

We start with the faith-conviction that, little as we know about God, he is love without limit. What he does for a world of men—whether we call his action creation, providence, grace, or salvation (and I do not mean to make them all the one)—is done freely on his part and undeservedly with respect to us, all in the direction of our fulfillment as free creatures. He would have us self-transcendently loving with respect to one another. Our destiny is to resemble him, to be like him in his self-giving love.

Jesus was a man of whom it was thought, after he was experienced as risen, that he was the high point of God's being with men. He represented to those who accepted him in faith the summit of agapean devotion. His living for others, even to death, was taken as a manifestation of God's presence such as had

---

29. **Epistola IV, PG** 3, 1072; the development in the above paragraph follows Schoonenberg, **The Christ,** pp. 59f.

never been in human history. Believers in him as the Son of God, the Christ, the Lord were convinced that in him "the complete being of the godhead dwells embodied, and in him you have been brought to completion" (Col 2, 9). In other words, not only is God's *plērōma* found in the person of Christ, but those who accept him may expect fulfillment on similar terms (*peplēromenoi*).

Theologians like Rahner and Schoonenberg, and religious thinkers like Teilhard de Chardin, see in Christ risen and to come the ultimate in human self-transcendence, a point reached by him not at once but in stages of development through his human history.[30] As glorified, he is what God eternally would have humanity to be. We shall be fulfilled in some sense as he is, though we have no clear idea of the "glory to be revealed in us" in the "revelation of the sons of God" (Rom 8, 18f.). If it is asked what prompted the first Christians to repose such faith in him, the answer must be that they had reasons sufficient for them. Some theologians maintain, as we have pointed out, that they possessed the concept of a divine man or a cosmic Christ and simply put Jesus of Nazareth in that role. This may be. Let us for the moment grant it. The point is that no other historical

---

30. Recent theological writing on the point would include Alois Grillmeier, "Christology," Sacramentum Mundi: An Encyclopedia of Theology, 3 (New York: Herder and Herder, 1969), 186-92; John Knox, The Humanity and Divinity of Christ (Cambridge: At the University Press, 1967); John McIntyre, The Shape of Christology: (London: SCM Press, 1966); John Macquarrie, "The Person of Jesus Christ," in Principles of Christian Theology (New York: Macmillan, 1966), pp. 246-79; "The Pre-existence of Jesus Christ," Expository Times 78 (October, 1966), 1-9; Karl Rahner, "Current Problems in Christology," Theological Investigations, I (Baltimore: Helicon, 1961), 149-200; "On the Theology of the Incarnation," ibid., IV (1966), 105-20; "Christology within an Evolutionary View," (ibid.), V, 57-92; "Jesus Christ. IV. History of Dogma and Theology," Sacramentum Mundi, 3, 192-209; Piet Schoonenberg, The Christ (New York: Herder and Herder, 1971); " 'He Emptied Himself,'. . . Philippians 2, 7," in Who Is Jesus of Nazareth? Concilium, Volume 11 (New York: Paulist Press, 1966), 47-66; Pierre Teilhard de Chardin, The Phenomenon of Man (New York: Harper, 1959); Hymn of the Universe (ibid., 1965); for literature in criticism of Teilhard's cosmic Christology, cf. Helmut Riedlinger, "The Universal Kingship of Christ," in Who Is Jesus of Nazareth? pp. 119-24; J.A.T. Robinson, The Human Face of God (London: SCM, 1973).

human being was ever suggested as having been such a one. His life both before and after his glorification was such that it was thought right to venerate him as Son of God and Savior.

Numerous contemporaries are uneasy at the attribution to him of any identification other than that of Israel's Messiah. This is a historically credible title, they hold, any other in the realm of divinity being mythical. But, of course, if anything other than literal Davidic kingship is meant, "Messiah" is equally mythical. It seems uncritical to put a limit on the way Jesus impressed those who knew him as the Christ, derived from modern convictions about what they should and should not have thought of him. The Isaian title Emmanuel was taken to be not without meaning, literal meaning, in the human history of Jesus (cf. Mt 1, 23.) Greeks and Jews tried to mythicize him subsequently, as for example in the pious elaborations of his power found in the canonical gospels or in the Johannine conception of the Son who was a man previously with the Father, come to earth and returned to the Father. The fourth gospel holds a gnosticizing tendency in check, but barely. The "false apostles" referred to by Paul in 1 and 2 Corinthians, and the second-century docetists, give free rein to it. The protection against such a tendency in Catholic orthodoxy was the conviction that the God among us was, at all points, *sarx*.

Modern Christology recognizes that "person" is a human term, representing what we know about the free and responsible if entirely mystifying beings that we ourselves are. Used with respect to God, it is analogous. Like anything we say of God, it is couched in unknowing and arrived at chiefly through removing the limitations that attend a human or creaturely conception. We are right, therefore, to say of God that he is "person" but only so long as we realize that we speak analogously. When we say that Jesus Christ was a person, a human person, we are both faithful to Scripture and using the term properly, not analogously. He was one person and not two, not a divine person and a human person. He was, however, a human person whose human nature was the special possession of the one divine person-nature, a man in intimate conjunction with God. By being so possessed, by being in such a union, this man Jesus lived a life that was the human life of God. He was one, not two; yet all that could be said of man could be said of him and all that could be said of God could be said of him. The union made him God's Son. It was effected by that power of God at work in the world which is called the "Holy Spirit" in the New Testament. It was effected in time. The mystery of God as Father, Son, and Spirit is a mystery of man's salvation in time.

The traditional doctrine of the Logos is a means to express the "expressive Being" of God, as distinct from the "primordial Being" of God, or the Father. In the creation and again in the Incarnation, God gives or spends himself in the way that is proper to him by nature. Looking from Christ back to the beginning of creation, believers in him say that all this is from God. Moreover, there is necessarily in God an eternal self-giving that is properly conveyed by the notion of a creative, expressive Logos. This Logos is eternal with the eternity of God himself. Expressed in time in Jesus Christ, it constitutes him the image of God and the prototype of all creation. Christ is he who "brings to actualization the potentialities for being that belong to creation."[31]

Is God, then, not triune eternally; are there not three substantial relations in his Being? Our only source, the New Testament does not answer that question. He may well be; but if we say that he has to be we have gone beyond the data. We have projected a mystery of God in time, in face of which we are barely at ease, onto the screen of eternity, where we are not at ease at all.

Would not such a Christology be Arian, declaring the Son a creature and holding for a time when he was not? No, because what is God in the Son is not a creature. God always was, and always was the God who through his expressed Logos would have a Son. This Son, come to birth, is to be adored as consubstantial with the Father.

Well, would it not be Nestorian with its two "persons," even if analogously such—the human person Jesus and the divine

---

31. Macquarrie, "The Pre-existence," col. 7.

person God? No, because this Christology maintains Christ's unity as person, which Ephesus affirmed against Nestorius, and rejects his duality of persons, which Ephesus denied. The important difference is, it does not have the same starting point as Cyril and the anti-Nestorian party, namely the one person of the incarnate Word. This assumption, set side by side with the man Jesus, makes two persons in Christ. Our Christology recognizes one person only, the person of Jesus of Nazareth.

But it has to be, if not Sabellian, modalist in some form or other. Sabellius was reprobated for saying that the Father became the Son to redeem us. For us, the Son is a man in time to whom the Father is uniquely present. Far from *being* the Father, he is Son to the Father.

Then the Trinity is an economic one, in that the Incarnation is viewed as a manifestation of God's power in time, the terms Son and Spirit having to do with God's work in time? Precisely, for that is what the New Testament makes of the mystery of God as Father, Son, and Spirit.

The recommendations of this Christology should be self-evident. First, it is completely faithful to the New Testament. It does not put a strain on full acceptance of it, as the post-Chalcedonian pseudo-orthodoxy developed from 451 to 600 does; this, because it does not begin from the non-scriptural starting point that the eternal Father has an eternal Son in the ontological sense. There is in God eternally a word, a wisdom, a plan, which comes to view in time.

Second, Jesus is credible as one of us, a matter imperilled by all Christologies in which the eternal Word "possesses a human nature." That nature remains in the popular mind a marionette, despite all efforts to declare it "free and creaturely before God" or to accord it a "psychological ego-center" which is not the same as an "ontological ego-center."[32]

Third, Jesus becomes supremely important to us because his

32. For a discussion and bibliography on this question, cf. Engelbert Gutwenger, "The Problem of Christ's Knowledge," in **Who Is Jesus of**

future was as hidden from him as ours is from us. He won the victory—God vindicated his trust in him—because he followed his human vocation to the end. In glory now he has come to human fulfillment but as *viator* he was unequivocally one of us—free of neither anxiety nor pain through being already a *comprehensor* or one with infused knowledge. His vision of God was that of the immediacy of openness to all that God would have him do.

Fourth, although not in fact a sinner, he was able to sin. If the Scriptural statement that he was tempted even as we are does not mean this, it means nothing. Necessarily, then, he was tempted sexually, a matter of terrible importance to today's men and women of all ages. The greatest human temptation is to idolatry or pride, but it may be some time before our age rediscovers this. Meantime, it has need of a Christ who will be of some help to it in its particular need.

Lastly, a Christology for our times will be the basis of a soteriology that is accomplished by the personal appropriation in faith of Jesus' saving words. Any theory of God's action which saves apart from human understanding and free acceptance of his overtures is useless in our age. Even the classic "deed of God in Christ," Jesus' death and resurrection—acceptance of which in faith was enough for Paul—has about it the ring of a mythical action "out there" that does not move many to believe in Jesus as saving for them. As it happens, the New Testament has numerous other soteriologies available, not least of which is that of the synoptics, appropriation of the parables and sayings of Jesus in particular. He was a wise teacher, a compassionate teacher, a man who made a God of love and justice credible. His words are reported as saving to his hearers. They are proving saving to hearers of today in the developed and adapted way in which the evangelists preserved them. For our contemporaries, Jesus may or may not have lived again. They are very relaxed about

Nazareth? pp. 91-105; Karl Rahner, "Dogmatic Reflections on the Knowledge and Self-Consciousness of Christ," in **Theological Investigations,** Vol. V, pp. 193-215; DS 3905.

the "Easter faith." But they are moved by his saving words, just as four centuries of Church Fathers moved men largely with Matthew and John, often taking their Paul or leaving him alone.

Those who know Rahner will recognize the elements of evolutionary self-transcendence and human openness to God that are present in this chapter. He holds, however, to an incarnation of a previously existent divine person until his essay, "Christology Within an Evolutionary View," where he seems to mute this in favor of the enfleshing of God's Logos, unspecified within the deity except as always able-to-be-expressed. Schoonenberg in his 130-page essay in *The Christ*, "God and Man, or God in Man?" is my master, although in not following him in the necessity of a "becoming God"—his favorable view of process theology— it may simply be that I do not understand why the revelation of the Incarnation requires that he be such.

As to any "novelty" of my view, it certainly has that with respect to post-Chalcedonian pseudo-orthodoxy.[33] But Rahner has reminded us of theology's important work as a history, not only of remembering what has been, but of forgetting.

---

33. A communication of the Congregation for the Doctrine of the Faith dated March 8, 1972, and released by Cardinal Francis Seper, but "ratified and confirmed" by Pope Paul VI at an audience of February 21, 1972, assumes the truth of certain matters that are subjected to question in this paper, namely, that it is divinely revealed that the Son of God was begotten before the ages **in his divine nature** and that the "persons" of the Most Holy Trinity are eternal. We repeat that both may very well be true as inner realities of the divine being but that the substance of the divine revelation on the Incarnation and the Trinity is something other. Papers such as this one are encouraged in The Declaration as part of the Church's duty to "examine the aforementioned mysteries constantly by contemplation and theological examination." Cf. **The Catholic Mind**, 70 (June, 1972), 61-64.

3   Irenaeus and the Future of Man

The lure and the dilemma of the Christian faith is the man Jesus. He both fascinates and frustrates, and for the same reason. Almost from the very beginning, men who talked about him talked also about God, and in the same breath. They felt they had to, to do justice to their own experience and conviction, and that has been both the lure and the dilemma. The New Testament documents exhibit a variety of ways of predicting both human and divine activity, or human and divine being, in Jesus. They range from the assertion that Jesus was a prophet through whom God was heralding the coming of the kingdom, or the belief that he had been assumed into heaven and would return again to usher in the end, to the full-blown claim that Jesus was a divine being who had participated in human existence and returned again to heaven. In any case, those who were captivated by him wondered in their several ways how to speak at once of the man and of God.

It is not surprising that the fathers of the Church did their most extensive and profound wondering about the manner in which Jesus could be said to be divine. That Jesus was a man was rarely ever formally denied, although practically the humanity was ignored, neglected, or given a purely formal treatment. At the heart of the trinitarian controversy was the problem of understanding how the Word who participated in the created world could be divine; or to put it otherwise, how to comprehend how God could both be present and not be present in the life and death of the man Jesus. For the doctrine of christology, the problem was how to assert humanity and divinity in Jesus without qualifying either. The church fathers did so at Chalcedon by speaking of the two natures of the one person Jesus. Within the bounds of the intellectual framework at their disposal, the settlement was an admirable and durable one, outlasting many generations of church fathers. It is evident, though, that the Chalcedonian formula embodies understandings of both God and man that have largely outlived their active apologetic usefulness. There is a kind of divine-human equation inherent in the claim that Jesus has both a human nature and a divine nature that seduces one into imagining that humanity and divinity are somehow comparable terms, so that when one speaks of Jesus' divine nature one has said something roughly equivalent to speaking of his human nature. That is to say, both our conception of divinity and our conception of humanity have changed. With the realization of our considerable ability to determine the careers of both the physical and psychic worlds, it has become necessary to rethink the dimensions and the definition of man. Whenever the balance between our conceptions of humanity and divinity is shifted by the dislocation of one or the other, the christological dilemma presents itself once more. Anthropology and christology are inseparably linked together.

In recent years the problem of the dimensions of christology has asserted itself more and more often. In ecumenical discussions one has heard a great deal about "cosmic christology,"[1] and the World Council itself, acting in response to that call, has determined that their own studies must first focus on an understanding of man. Nothing has happened to Christ. It is man, having visited the moon and having stolen secrets from stars and atoms alike, who is beginning to suspect his own cosmic dimensions and absolute involvement with the natural world around and within him. And if Christ has to do with the redemption of such men as we find ourselves to be, then in some sense, he too must be "cosmic."

---

1. The speech by Joseph Sittler at the New Delhi Assembly of the World Council of Churches in 1961 is still the clearest and best argument for rethinking christology in a context as large as man's own involvements, which involvements already reach from the heart of atomic things out to the moon and beyond. See "Called to Unity" in **The Ecumenical Review**, XIV (January, 1962), 177-87.

Whether or not one is comfortable with terms like "cosmic christology," it is undeniably the case that the whole issue of the relationship of anthropology to christology is at stake. Christian tradition is not without resource for clarification of that problem, and it is to one of the most interesting fathers of the church I propose to turn. This relationship of anthropology to christology appears with pointed clarity in the writings of Irenaeus, one of the first theologians to have a conscious doctrine of man. It was undoubtedly the pressure of gnostic understandings of the human condition that caused Irenaeus to center on anthropology in this way, and that might be the subject of another study. Not only is his a conscious anthropology, but because Irenaeus' understanding of man was not the norm for his time, it is surprisingly suggestive for our own time.

First, his definition of man is in developmental, not formal, terms. One must believe, Irenaeus said, that there is a God who has made and fashioned everything, bringing it out of nothing.[2] Man was the intended aim of God's creative activities, and the cosmos was made for him.[3] The Son of God, one of God's "hands," was the image and likeness of God, and was himself the instrument by which God created all things.[4] Man, who was not himself the image and likeness of God, was *created in* the image and likeness of God by the Son (who was uncreated), in order that even the visible appearance of man should reflect his creator as much as possible.

Taking the purest and finest of earth, Irenaeus wrote, God mingled his own power with the created stuff of the universe,

---

2. Irenaeus, **Proof of Apostolic Preaching**, trans. by Joseph P. Smith, in **Ancient Christian Writers, No. 16** (Westminster, Maryland: Newman Press, 1952), Sect. 4. Hereinafter referred to as **Proof** 4, etc.

3. Irenaeus, **Against Heresies**, in **The Ante-Nicene Fathers, V. 1**, ed. by Roberts and Donaldson (Grand Rapids, Michigan: Eerdmans, 1953). Reprint of the 1885 edition. 5.29.1. (Hereinafter referred to as AH 5.29.1, etc.)

4. **Proof** 11, AH 4.38.9, AH 4.33.4

and breathed his own inspiration into man;[5] and the woman was made from man. "Adam and Eve (for this was the name of the woman) were naked and were not ashamed," Irenaeus said, "for their thoughts were innocent and childlike, and they had no conception or imagination of the sort that is engendered in the soul by evil. . . . For they were in their integrity, preserving their natural state. . . . For this reason they were not ashamed, as they kissed each other and embraced in the innocence of childhood."[6] According to Irenaeus, when God created him, man was a kind of child who had a long way to go before he might reach perfection. "The man," he says, "was a little one; for he was a child and had need to grow so as to come to his full perfection."[7] The childhood of Adam to which Irenaeus here refers, and which is so important for his whole theological position, is not just a simple physical immaturity. Rather, Irenaeus believed that man, when he was created, was not yet what he later was to become. The childhood of Adam was not so much a case of the man being young in years, although it was that, too; it was that man*kind* was immature, undeveloped, and in some sense, not yet even properly man.[8] Even so, man—Adam—was made Lord of the earth and everything in it. And so that he might have nourishment and grow up in luxury, God prepared a place for him better than this world, well-favored in climate, beauty, and all other needful things, and God walked around and talked with Adam, prefiguring what was to come in the future when he would become man's fellow and come among mankind.

That mankind was like a child at creation is basic to Irenaeus' thinking, and directly instructive for his doctrines of man and christology. The essential difference between God and man is that God is uncreated, and that man is created. To be created, according to Irenaeus, is to be new, young, and immature. It is

---

5. Proof 11.
6. Proof 14.
7. Proof 12.
8. AH 4.39.2.

the nature of created things to grow and to develop. Adam and Eve, he said, "having been created a short time previously," had not the faintest idea how to procreate children.[9] Irenaeus wondered if God might not have, at the beginning, created a perfect (that is, mature) man. It was not possible, he decided, for the reason that all created things are inferior to the one who created them; and the Creator is perfect. Since there was, only recently, a time when man was not, man is created, and inasmuch as he is created, and not creator, he is less than perfect. Since all created things are, in relation to the Uncreated One, of later date, "so are they infantile."[10] The imperfection of the created man, even before he sinned, was not a fault in man, but only a recognition of his natural lack of development. "God," Irenaeus said, "had the power at the beginning to grant perfection to man; but as the latter was only recently created, he could not possibly have received it, or even if he had received it, could he have contained it, or containing it, could he have retained it."[11] As a boy is not yet a man, man at creation was not yet what he was destined to become. As a boy is not reprehensible for not yet having become a full-grown man, neither was mankind at creation blameworthy for not yet being what man should later become. According to Irenaeus, growth and development is the characteristic of created being.[12] Growth, indeed, is the continuing creative activity of God.[13] What is notable in Irenaeus' discussion of Adam is that he put the emphasis on what God intended in Adam, and not just on the Fall. Here is a dynamic anthropology, invested with the growth and potential of man.

In the second place, then, and as a result of his developmental view of man, *the fall into sin is not a fall from perfection, but a frustration of growth.* The Garden with its well-favored climate

---

9. AH 3.22.4.
10. AH 4.38.1.
11. AH 4.38.2.
12. AH 2.28.1.
13. AH 4.39.2.

notwithstanding, Adam (or man) sinned. "The man," Irenaeus explained, "was a little one, and his discretion still undeveloped, wherefore also he was easily misled by the deceiver."[14] God had laid down certain conditions for man, so that if he kept them he would remain as he was, without death; but Adam sinned, and death corrupted the creation.[15] Man was created to grow in the image and likeness of God. Growth was given by God, and sin was an arresting of God-given growth. The terms Irenaeus uses to describe the Fall are terms from adolescence, telling of the perversion of man's intended development. Sin, happening as it did at the very beginning of the development of man, meant not only that man would not grow into the image and likeness of God—that is, into immortality—but also would frustrate his becoming man.[16]

Because Adam was created to be the lord of creation, his sin had effect on the rest of creation, and the earth brought forth thorns and thistles.[17] As Irenaeus regarded him, man is not an alien on the earth. He *is* earth, made alive by the Spirit of God, and he belongs to the earth. "Adam was molded from this earth to which we belong. . . ."[18] There are, for Irenaeus, only two basic kinds of things. There is God who alone is uncreated, and there is the creation; and man is a part and the lord of creation. What affects man affects the rest of creation. What man effects, affects creation. Just so, then, when Irenaeus speaks of the work of Christ who became man, he speaks often of his participation in, and use and redemption of, the creation.[19] By his refusal to regard man as a spiritual as opposed to a material being,[20] Irenaeus demonstrated the seriousness with which he identified man as an integral part of the created order. There is no hint in his theology

---

14. Proof 12.
15. Proof 15, AH 5.16.1, AH 5.2.
16. AH 4.39.2.
17. Proof 17.
18. AH 5.16.1.
19. See, for instance, AH 5.2.2, 5.33.1, 5.36.1, 5.33.3, 5.36.3.
20. AH 5.6.1.

that the ultimate destiny of man rests in his liberation from his essential earthliness, not that his sin consists of his earthliness. As we shall soon see, man's redemption and the redemption of the world are organically one. Adam without his earthliness is not Adam.

The Son of God was the image and likeness of God, and man was created by the Son to grow to be like that image and likeness; not however to *become* the image and likeness. That man sinned meant that he stopped growing to be like the Son, and in effect, arrested the intended course of God's creative activity. It meant that man frustrated his destiny to become like the Son.[21] In order, then that the intention of God in creation not be forever abandoned, the Son himself became man to recapitulate his own work, and destroy the death that was corrupting the creation.

Third, then, the incarnation is the resumption and attainment of true humanity. "Recapitulation" is probably the term most characteristic of Irenaeus, and it has a dual meaning. The word is used to suggest both a recovery of an original, and a bringing of something to completion. Because of these two kinds of images inherent in Irenaeus' use of the term, it is sometimes supposed that Irenaeus was not consistent, or even that the writings do not represent a single theology.[22] But it is precisely here that much of the uniqueness of Irenaeus' position is evident. Had Irenaeus held the view that God, in the beginning, had made a finished and perfect creation, then the fall into sin would have been a kind of subtraction from perfection. The redemption of the world, in that case, would have been a matter of restoring the world to its original perfection. To the contrary, Irenaeus never speaks of man or the creation as perfect, except when referring to Christ. That is not to say that he regarded the work of God as something less than perfect in the sense that it was inferior. Man and the

---

21. AH 2.28.1, 4.38.3.
22. See Gustaf Wingren, **Man and the Incarnation**, trans. by Ross Mackenzie (Philadelphia: Muhlenberg Press, 1959), pp. 26ff.

world are imperfect, first because they are created and not creator, and second, because they were still becoming.

Man, as God created him, was only at the beginning of his intended development. Man, according to Irenaeus, was created to grow to maturity from the childhood of his origins to the full development that time would bring. Since man is a created being, and by definition not inherently perfect, he has to grow *toward* perfection.[23] Sin interrupted man's God-given growth, and redemption in Christ was a resumption of that growth into the image and likeness of God.[24] By his entrance into the human situation, Christ began afresh God's creative activity, beginning again, so to speak, where development had stopped: right at the beginning.[25] It was, then, both the recovery of the original state, and a bringing of man's growth to completion. The operative image is that of growth.[26]

Irenaeus contrasts the two Adams: the original, and Christ. He believed that Christ "summing up afresh"[27] every stage in the development of man, from childhood to old age, recapitulated the whole career of man. Christ, he said, was an infant for infants, a child for children, a youth for youths, and an old man for old men.[28] At about forty years of age, Irenaeus thought, a man begins to decline toward old age. Since Jesus was questioned whether he, who was not yet fifty years of age, had seen Abraham, Irenaeus supposed that Jesus was more than forty, but not yet quite fifty years of age.[29] Christ was a new Adam, not in the sense that he was another, separate creation of God, but in that he was an undistorted resumption of the original intention and creation of God.[30] "When he became incarnate, and was made man," Irenaeus

---

23. AH 4.38.1.
24. AH 3.18.1.
25. AH 3.18.7.
26. AH 3.19.1.
27. **Proof** 32.
28. AH 2.22.2, 2.22.4, 2.22.6, 3.18.7.
29. AH 2.22.5, 2.22.6.
30. AH 3.22.10, 5.3.2.

wrote, "he commenced afresh the long line of human beings, and furnished us, in a brief, comprehensive manner, with salvation; so that what we had lost in Adam—namely, to be according to the image and likeness of God—that we might recover in Christ Jesus."[31]

Anthropology and christology hang very closely together in Irenaeus' theology, and they do so consciously. Man is a growing, developing, and still unfinished creature. Sin is turning from the one who gives life and growth; a process of dying. Sin is the frustration of the life and growth of man toward man-ness. What happens to man in Christ is the continuation of the work of creation. Redemption is not restoration to a previously realized state, but is resumption of the development toward true humanity. Again, it is not the destiny of man to become God; it is rather for man to become man. In Christ the intention of God for man is evident and complete. The recapitulation (or redemption) of man *is* the creation of man and the completion and clarification of the creation.[32] In a sense, Irenaeus was making his way between the notion of development on the one side and restoration on the other. The Lord "commenced afresh the long line of human beings." What was intended to develop at the beginning, and didn't, begins again; and Jesus is the way it happens. The original intention is restored in him.[33] That is the double meaning of recapitulation, of course.

Fourth, man, and the world as nature, are so interrelated that man cannot be conceived of apart from history and nature. That is, the nature and destiny of man are inseparable from the nature and destiny of the rest of creation. Man, Irenaeus said, real man, is a very earthly creature. He is made from the things of the earth, and his destiny is here. He was made free, his own master, created

---

31. AH 3.18.1.
32. AH 4.39.2.
33. See Norbert Brox, **Offenbarung, Gnosis und gnostischer Mythos bei Irenaeus von Lyon** (Verlag Anton Pustet, Salzburg und Muenchen, 1966), pp. 186-87.

to be the master of everything on earth.[34] Irenaeus recognized that one might speak of the spirit and soul of man, but perfect man is not a spiritual being. He is body, soul, and spirit. Were one to take from man the substance of the flesh, Irenaeus said, which is itself the handiwork of God, what would be left would not be a spiritual man, but merely the spirit of man. When the spirit of God is poured into the body and soul of man, then is there a man as God created him. "Now the soul and the spirit are certainly a *part* of the man," he said, "but certainly not *the* man."[35]

The place of the physical universe, of physical man, is important for Irenaeus' understanding of man and Christ. Man cannot be conceived of apart from the created stuff of the world, and both the sin of man and his redemption have a great deal to do with the well-being of the world as a physical place.

The recapitulation of man was the recapitulation of the *whole* man. "Some affirm," Irenaeus said, "that neither their soul nor their body can receive eternal life, but merely the inner man. . . . Others [maintain] . . . that while the soul is saved, their body does not participate in the salvation that comes from God."[36] But man, and not merely a *part* of man, is saved. The saved man is a complete man, body and soul.[37] Because man is a created being, he is incapable of realizing the presence and activity of God, except as it is evident in created things. It is by means of the creation itself that the Word reveals God; by means of the world that the Lord is revealed to be the maker of the world.[38] "Vain in every respect," he said, "are they who despise the entire dispensation of God, and disallow the salvation of the flesh. . . ."[39] "If the flesh did not attain incorruption," Irenaeus continued,

---

34. **Proof** 11, 12, AH 5.16.1, 5.2.2.
35. AH 5.6.1.
36. AH 5.19.2.
37. AH 5.20.1, 5.6.1.
38. AH 4.6.6.
39. AH 5.2.2.

"then neither did the Lord renew us with his blood . . . nor [is] the bread which we break the communion of his body. For the blood can only come from veins and flesh, and whatsoever else makes up the substance of man. . . . And as we are his members, we are also nourished by means of the creation."[40] Inasmuch as Christ has acknowledged wine (a part of creation) to be his blood, and bread (also a part of creation) to be his body, salvation is inseparable from physical being. For that reason Irenaeus can claim that the final result of the work of the Spirit is the salvation of the flesh.[41] If it were not that, it would be a salvation of something other than man. In latter days the pre-existent Son of God appeared as man, "resuming anew in himself all things in heaven and on earth."[42] Referring to Christ's promise to drink wine with his disciples in his Father's kingdom, Irenaeus said that the passage cannot in any manner be understood as referring to a super-celestial place: drinking wine is something that flesh and blood people do.[43]

There is a dogged determination in Irenaeus' theology not to talk of man, his future, or his salvation as occuring anywhere other than in connection with the earth from which he was made. Since man and the earth itself both are created, and since man is himself earthly stuff breathed into life, the recapitulation or renewed development of man is at the same time a renewal of the whole creation. The creation is the place where God is seen, and with the restoration of man, is itself renewed.[44] The restored creation will, when man has himself grown to maturity, once more be his dominion, in perfect subjection to him. *Finally, Irenaeus is a thoroughly biblical theologian.* In his book, *The Biblical Theology of St. Irenaeus,* John Lawson asserted that it was his aim to show the biblical character of Irenaeus' work.[45] It is scarcely to be

---

40. AH 5.2.2.
41. AH 5.12.4.
42. Proof 30.
43. AH 5.33.1.
44. AH 5.32.1.
45. (London: Epworth Press, 1948), pp. 18-19.

doubted. The language, data, and relational structures of his theology are all drawn from the Bible. What is of particular importance for this paper is not Irenaeus' general saturation with the biblical thought world, evident on nearly every page of his work, but the biblical character of what is most peculiarly unique to his theology.

Even the term "recapitulation," which characterizes his christology, is a biblical word. It is taken from Ephesians 1:10, and represents Irenaeus' attempt to embody the whole of the biblical proclamation about the work of Christ in a single word:[46] "that he would bring everything together under Christ, as head, everything in the heavens and everything on earth." The main theme of Ephesians is to show how the whole body of creation, cut off from the creator by sin, is degenerating, and that its rebirth is made possible as Christ re-unites the whole creation as his body with himself as its head. This theme of the creation-wide effect of redemption is obviously central to Irenaeus' thought. The same massive scope of redemption is evident in Colossians 1:15-20. Following the form of Eduard Schweitzer's reconstruction[47] the passage reads:

I

He is the image of the unseen God
and the first-born of all creation,
for in him were created
all things in heaven and on earth:
all things were created through him and for him.

II

Before anything was created, he existed,
and he holds all things in unity,
and he is the head of the body.*

---

46. Wingren, **Man and the Incarnation**, p. 8.

III

And he is the beginning
he was the first to be born from the dead,
because God wanted all perfection
to be found in him
and all things to be reconciled through him.[48]

The phrase, "he is the head of the body," in stanza II, which seems to suggest the church (and is interpreted that way in its later literary form), probably does not refer to the church at all. Both the first and second stanzas refer to the creation, not to redemption. It is more likely that "body" refers to the cosmos. To speak of the Logos as the head of the universe was not an uncommon Hellenistic usage.[49] In stanza III, the term *pleroma* is a matter of some dispute. It is translated here, "God wanted *all perfection* to be found in him"; sometimes, "For in him *all the fullness of God* was pleased to dwell." It probably refers to the entirety of the cosmos, rather than to the entirety of God's attributes.[50] That is to say, the fullness of God's being-in-the-world is focused in Christ, and all things are reconciled through him.

This same New Testament theme of the redemption of everything in creation is also evident in Romans 8:22-23: "From the beginning till now the entire creation, as we know, has been groaning in one great act of giving birth, and not only creation, but all of us. . . ." There is no New Testament christology: there are a variety of New Testament christologies. It is plain that this particular Pauline emphasis found a ready proponent in Irenaeus. In other respects, his biblical foundations are clear. But even at that point where Irenaeus seems most outside the characteristic christological tradition of the church—that is, the complete seri-

---

48. This translation is from the Jerusalem Bible (London: Darton, Longmans and Todd, 1966), with the exception of the line marked°, which is Fuller's translation.

49. Fuller, **Foundations of New Testament Christology**, p. 215.

50. **Ibid.** See also the Jerusalem Bible, which agrees with Fuller.

ousness with which he encompasses literally all things in redemption, and not just man—even at that point he represents a genuinely biblical tradition not generally reflected in western theologies.

There is a close and necessary relationship between one's understanding of man, and one's understanding of christology. The dimensions of christology are affected by the dimensions of the man who is redeemed. To say the very least, christology cannot be smaller than the man to be redeemed, or else redemption is a partial thing. If man is an alien on the earth, better liberated from it, then christology might indeed confine itself to that part of man to be rescued from his earthliness. If, on the other hand, as Irenaeus suggested, man is inconceivable apart from his place on the earth, if redemption must be as wide as the reach of man, then Christ must have something to do also with the heavens and the earth.

In the early church, as is evident in such biblical passages as we have mentioned, a creation-wide redemption was considered possible by demonstrating that in Jesus one had to do with the eternal, pre-existent One in whom the cosmos came to be, and in whom it exists. That was in no way to deny Jesus' humanity: it was to think of and explain the significance of his life and death in terms of his divinity. I suggest that today we must do quite the opposite. If we cannot think of and explain the importance of Jesus for us and for our world precisely and primarily in terms of his humanity, it will be just so much mysterious talk about redeemed people and redeemed stars, and few will be able to take it seriously. We realize today, in a way never before recognized so painfully, that what goes on in people's heads has a great deal to do with other people, and with the moon and the stars, too; what they shall become, and even whether they shall continue to be. It is not possible, today, to conceive of man *without* thinking at the same time of his place in the developing universe, and of the potentiality that man has to enhance or to ruin the world that gave birth to him and that nourishes him. We cannot consistently think of our own redemption apart from the world, not because Christ pre-existed, but because if he became man, he became a man inextricably bound up with a world. There is no other kind of man.

The recognition that man is more than he ever was, and not yet what he shall be, has profound effect upon the formulation of christological doctrine. It is no longer possible for us to believe that once at creation we were perfect, and that as a consequence we are now less than we were. We are still becoming what we shall become. We are unscrambling the genetic code that shapes what man biologically shall become, we are probing into space, and we are acquiring socially manipulative data of all kinds. The horrible and tantalizing realization that the futures of both man and nature are in our own hands is just now sifting down to the conscious places in our lives. So for us redemption is not something other than creation, but a new possibility for a creation still happening; and the new possibility must be a historical possibility. Irenaeus did speak of Christ in just that way. It may be that this aspect of Irenaeus' thought is more accessible to us today than it was to his contemporaries. He was one of the first (if not the first) theologians to work out a christology in conscious awareness of a doctrine of man; a doctrine of a man created with purpose, in time, within which man in the image of God has reason, freedom, and the moral responsibility to become human; but also a man who fails. If we are such men, then redemption may indeed be what Irenaeus suggested it is: a new possibility for man to realize his own humanity.

A pertinent christology demands an articulate doctrine of man.

4 American Indian Religion: Sacred, Secular, Human

CARL F. STARKLOFF

We might begin our discussion with Kipling's noble phrase, "The White Man's Burden." But I use it in a different sense, being well aware that what once seemed an expression of the mission of European Christianity to offer civilization to the heathen now rings more in our ears to the accompaniment of a much older saying, "They bind heavy burdens and lay them on men's shoulders, without being willing to lift even a finger to move them." It is now pretty clear who has wound up bearing the white man's burden. And yet, we whites do still have a burden, even though it so often rides on the shoulders of other peoples—the burden of a culture (not necessarily evil, and certainly having many blessings!) for which a people was not prepared, and which leads that people more and more toward a complete loss of its own origins and traditions.

This is not intended to be a guilt-sermon; guilt is paralyzing. My point is rather that members of white society must be ready to encourage modern Indians to reach back to a time when their culture was whole, as far as this is possible, and give this people a chance to do its own developing, perhaps away from older traditions, perhaps back to some of them in their purity. Is this idea realistic at this late date? My answer is a resounding *Yes!*, for at least three reasons. The first of these is the simple evidence of revival of American Indian traditions in many areas of the country, of certain religious ceremonies which even trained anthropologists predicted would disappear long before now. My second reason explains why I think that this is good: when we have lost something important, we go back to where we last had it. In the case of the Indian, he last had a sense of identity, of "being at the center of the world," when he had an intact tribal religious culture. My own phrase "reaching back" seemed inadequate to me in defending this position, and I was delighted to come upon a much happier statement in some recent reading: historian Bernard Sheehan, after a long discussion of culture conflict between White and Indian, is not sure whether the Indian tradition can survive or not. Perhaps the Indian of history will indeed die a tragic death, but Sheehan asks that it be a death with integrity: "If his death is to be tragic, it must be the death of his real self, not of a white imposter."[1]

My third reason for my position is theological and pastoral. If all that St. Paul says about the universality of Christianity is valid, then the subjection of Christ to any one culture is gross idolatry. The Church has its being in Jesus Christ alone, who as a man lived in one culture but who now depends on no culture and can thus live in any of them. As a Christian, I must recognize that faith and/or religion, depending on whose definitions we use, are not to be identified with culture, and that faith can live in every culture because its origin is in Spirit. Indian culture nurtures the religious spirit in these people, and, in accord with the theme of this volume, Indian religion leads them to a noble form of human existence.

Hartley Burr Alexander is certainly accurate when he grants the presence in North American Indian religion of grosser elements and brutalities, of often misguided enthusiasm and bestiality, as we find in all societies where religious enthusiasm occurs.[2] But we have Alexander's positive testimony to the nobility of these traditions, as well as that of Joachim Wach, who wrote about the famous secret societies among Indian tribes, detailing such qualities as genuine experience of the holy, the fostering of awe

---

1. Bernard W. Sheehan, "Indian-White Relations in Early America," in Francis Paul Prucha, ed., **The Indian in American History** (New York: Holt, Rinehart and Winston, 1971), pp. 51-66. Cf. pg. 66.

2. Hartley Burr Alexander, **The World's Rim** (Lincoln: University of Nebraska Press, 1969), p. 231.

and reverence, stress upon careful preparation, ascetic discipline of mind and body, meditation and solitude. Wach believed that Indian religious associations were superior to other primitive groups—less purely pragmatic in aspiration, of loftier and more subtle conception, more sober in practice, subject to more rigid discipline. Indian prophets show a sense of divine initiative in their roles. They schooled themselves in suffering and solitude, and were such men as to command the ear and respect of their fellow tribesmen.[3]

There is a tendency, born of white America's nostalgia, often helped along by what Ernst Cassirer called the mischievous wiles of Indian interpreters who were having some fun with the white-eyes,[4] to romanticize and sentimentalize Indian culture. Indian religion has produced, proportionately, probably not too many more saints than any other religions have. And today, a visit to any reservation should not be expected to yield immediate visions of a lofty tribal culture; the first impression, and maybe even the second or third, could even make the visitor very depressed. But the point is that Indian religion need not be sentimentalized; it rides high on its own merits. We need only read such works as those of Alexander,[5] or the personal testimonies of Black Elk, to appreciate the advanced development of religious and philosophical concepts in Indian tradition. And where these are present, I submit, man is more human because he is more a child of God. As further reading would, I hope, illustrate, he is also more poetic and esthetically aware.

To a scholar like Bleeker, religion is its own source and begins of itself; it is not the product of other sources, social, esthetic or otherwise.[6] The simple religious person would merely say that

---

3. Joachim Wach, **Sociology of Religion** (Chicago: The University of Chicago Press, 1967 Phoenix Books Edition), pp. 117-119.

4. Ernst Cassirer, **Language and Myth**, trans. Susanne K. Langer (New York: Dover Publications, Inc., No date), pp. 68-69.

5. In addition to **The World's Rim**, see also Alexander's **North American Mythology** (Cambridge, Mass., The University Press, 1916).

6. C. J. Bleeker, "The 'Entelecheia' of Religious Phenomena," in

being a child of God comes first. Joachim Wach has written,

> Religion is sound and true to its nature only as long as it has no aim or purpose except the worship of God. Yet, wherever genuine religious experience as the concentration and direction of the best that is in man speaks, nuclei are formed which are integrated into a close unit primarily by what they consider holy.[7]

Men first relate to their Ground of Being, or their Living Centre, and then to one another—a position shared also by Martin Buber and St. Paul. Thus, religion is social as well as individuating, but the relation of the individual to the Other, the Divine Other, is primary. Here is where radical individuation takes place, and we need not and must not appeal to other benefits of the religious experience to validate it. But the individuation of faith response is man's humanization as well, as we see demonstrated in Indian tradition.

INDIVIDUATION THROUGH FAITH RESPONSE

One way or another, when a person listens to God, he has to stand out from the crowd to do it. This is where religion begins, and it is also where humanity begins—in individuation. The best known phenomenon of the person's transcendence in American Indian religion is the nearly extinct one of the holy man. Whether it can revive or not is an open question. But we do have records of the experiences of Indian prophets, thanks in large part to Black Elk's determination to pass on his testimony through Joseph Epes Brown and John Neihardt. It was to men like Black Elk that visions came, whether in dreams or solitary wanderings in the hills; in such men the Divine broke into this world. The first vision came to Black Elk as a boy of nine, and characteristically it lifted him out of his body to show him what must be, and then

---

Walter H. Capps, **Ways of Understanding Religion** (New York: The Macmillan Co., 1972), p. 155.

---

7. Wach, Op. Cit., p. 381.

sent him back to help his people in their contest for survival.[8]

The matter of visions and prophecies is a delicate one, and this is not the time to go into it. It is enough, I think, to say that if one applies the criteria of authors like Karl Rahner, Joseph Marechal and R. C. Zaehner to American Indian prophetism, prescinding from peyote-induced experiences (which is another whole new problem!), Indian history in this area emerges as empirically sound as that of other great religious traditions.[9] A study of the tragic nineteenth century history of North American life shows us a mystique of suffering and the power to endure it, thanks to religious conviction, that takes second place to none. It often calls to mind, in fact, the pathos, the stubbornness and the humor of the homeless Jew down through history. It may be only the deep religious traditions that have prevented their intense suffering from destroying the Indian people. Without it, their situation has resulted in tragedy for the individual and often tribal extinction; in place of religion there prevail alcoholism, inertia, despair, an alarming suicide rate. Scott Momaday's Pulizer Prize novel, *House Made of Dawn,* is a moving illustration of these conditions. On the other hand, where religious tradition has persevered, so has hope, and so has a sense of gradual progress within tribal tradition, nurtured and inspired by outstanding religious leaders. Alexander wrote,

Many are the Indian prophets, innovators of religion; and Indian tradition abounds in tales of vision-seekers, men who have gone into

---

8. Cf. Black Elk, **Black Elk Speaks,** as told to John G. Neihardt (Lincoln: University of Nebraska Press, 1961). This volume is the full life story of this mission. For further accounts by Black Elk, see Joseph Epes Brown, **The Sacred Pipe: Black Elk's Account of the Seven Rites of the Oglala Sioux** (Norman: University of Oklahoma Press, 1970).

9. For studies of visions and revelations, cf. Karl Rahner, "Visions and Prophecies," **Inquiries** (New York: Herder and Herder, 1964), pp. 87-188; Joseph Marechal, **Studies in The Psychology of the Mystics,** trans. Alger Thorold (New York: The Benziger Press, 1927); R.C. Zaehner, Mysticism, Sacred and Profane (London: Oxford University Press, 1967 paperback ed.).

the wilderness to meditate, seeking new light upon the problems of
life and bringing new revelations to their people.[10]

Veterans of the Arapaho Offerings Lodge ceremony bear witness
that suffering is unavoidable: they take no food or water for
three days and nights, and endure the day's heat and the night's
cold, for themselves and for the tribe.[11] In this way they might
be purified enough to be open to a vision from Man-Above.[12]
Endurance means a very pragmatic kind of strength for the Indian;
borne ritualistically it symbolizes the stamina of past times of
prairie life and creates a Now-Event of the tribe's history and
its relationship to Father-Above. Somehow, in the Offerings Lodge,
during what is called commonly "The Sun Dance," the experience
occurs that is beyond daily routine: "You think a lot in there,
and you cry a lot too," they say. You cry, and not just because
it hurts. Call it what you will, sentimentality on my part, or the
gift of tears, but I recall weeping as I witnessed the dance of the
rising sun, and the dance called "gambling against the sun" at the
close of the Offerings Lodge. It made me feel especially good
to see how for many white visitors the foolish legend of the stu-
pidly stolid and unblinking Indian vanished in a shared moment
of religious and human emotion. To pray "the Indian way" is to
experience religion as Kierkegaard's "infinite passion." Let me
cite an Arapaho Rabbit Lodge prayer, taken from Dorsey's account:

> Please, Father, Man-Above, do not get impatient at our constant
> prayers. You caused the cedar tree to grow and from it we get leaves
> for our incense for this pure water.
> Come and live with us, you Spirits, Supernatural-Beings, and
> help us in our supplications! We have boiled this water; placed the
> root and eating berries upon it, and it is now prepared. Poor and
> humble as we are in this world, surrounded by white people, please
> do have mercy upon us! May this cloud of smoke (incense) reach your
> nostrils, My Father and my Grandmother! Let our circuits (the courses

---

10. Alexander, Op. Cit., p. 171.
11. The idea of vicarious suffering is dominant in Arapaho rituals and
asceticism. Evidence based on personal conversations.
12. Cf. Alexander, Op. Cit., Ch. VI, "The Sun Dance."

with the sun, during the day) be firm, and free from accidents!

My Grandfather, Big-Painted-Red-Robe, listen to me! You are the one who directed and instructed me; and whatever I do, may it be pleasing to your sight! I have taken great pains to pursue the way which you gave me. May this woman (a wife of one participant) carry this kettle of sweet water safely to your holy place! As the geese drank that pure water without difficulty, so let it be with us! My Father, please come and be with us![13]

It is in such fervent prayer as this that Alexander admires the Indian's sense of closeness to the natural and spiritual world, calling not on the cruel deities of Greek religion, but on ultimate benevolence.[14] Suffering is permitted because the purpose of life is to prove the individual human soul.

Perhaps the most stabilizing belief for the traditional Indian, both individually and tribally, is the sense of the whole, of living "at the center of the earth." One sees this evidenced in communal ceremonies. The Offerings Lodge Pole is the Center, the sign of the Omphalos, the Tree of Life, the Place (in the religious sense) where clock time is transcended and origin myths are re-enacted. The reader may recall how the Cheyennes in "Little Big Man" called themselves the "Human Beings" who still live at the center of the universe, which white men have lost. In Arapaho mythology, Father-Above, the Creator, gives the center of the earth to the Arapahoes, whose original name, *Hinaneina,* means "Our People."[15] An Arapaho religious leader told me once about the

---

13. George A. Dorsey, **The Arapaho Sun Dance: The Ceremony of The Offerings Lodge** (Chicago: Field Columbian Museum Publication 75, Anthropological Series, Vol. IV, 1903), p. 148.

14. Alexander, Op. Cit., p. 199.

15. Cf. Virginia Cole Trenholm, **The Arapahoes, Our People** (Norman: University of Oklahoma Press, 1970), p. vii. For an alternative meaning to this word, spelled **inunaina**, see Tom Shakespeare, **The Sky People** (New York: Vantage Press, 1971), p. 19. Shakespeare gives his people the title of the book: "Sky People," but indicates pg. 54 that "human" meant simply "Our People" to ancient Arapahoes. For further comments on tribes with names of similar meaning, Cf. C. Scott Littleton on Georges Dumezil, "Tripartitism in Indo-European Mythology," in Capps, Op. Cit., pp. 161-162.

four shrines that mark off the Wind River Reservation and make it a place where "Our People" can dwell under divine providence. Eliade calls it the myth of "sacred space."[16] Is it also a case of a primitive racist arrogance? As originally understood, not at all. What the myth says is that I the individual and we the community, live where God has chosen for us to live, and only prophecy or catastrophe will move us very far away. We are His people, and because of this we know where we are. Let others also do the same, for, as Black Elk said to John Neihardt, "Anywhere is the center of the world."[17] When you stand at the Center, you are an individual. This is the myth of the Center!

We might sum up this part of the discussion with the current cliché about the Indian and his sensitivity to nature and his ecological sense, his closeness to his own body, to nature, to the earth.[18] This may be overdone now, but it is no empty fairy tale. Indians have had to possess this awareness, and they still do wherever tradition is kept. It is not a "love affair with nature"; it is a *real* affair, a relationship in which not only warm emotion but also terror and grief confront man. A sense of the Whole encounters not only the divine but the demonic. In nature, the spirits lie waiting, and man must not treat nature as a mere thing; he is called to *address* nature. Thus we read or hear sacramental prayers to the Four Old Men (the Winds), to Grandmother the Moon, Grandfather the Sun, Mother Earth, Old Woman the Night, and all the spirits, the messengers of Ichebbeniathan— Man-Above, who is Our Father.[19]

---

16. Mircea Eliade, **The Sacred and The Profane,** trans. Willard R. Trask (New York: Harper and Row, Torchbook ed. 1961), Ch. I.

17. Black Elk, Op. Cit., p. 43.

18. I have discussed this elsewhere, with further references. Cf. Carl F. Starkloff, "American Indian Religion and Christianity: Confrontation and Dialogue," **Journal of Ecumenical Studies,** Vol. 8, No. 2, Spring, 1971, pp. 317-340; reprinted in Martin E. Marty and Dean G. Peerman, ed., **New Theology** No. 9 (New York: Macmillan Co., 1972), pp. 121-150. See footnotes 8 and 46.

19. References to these titles are scattered throughout Dorsey's work **The Arapaho Sun Dance,** cited above.

THE ARTICULATION OF MYTHS

It may be that the most significant contribution Indian religion could make to a society in which individuation suffers so painfully is the ability to articulate meaningful myths about our deepest hopes and fears. Carl Jung wrote about the primitive mentality (and this is not just in aborigines or in past ages!) that it does not *invent* myths but *experiences* them in revelations of the preconscious. Myths are the primitive mental life, the living heritage of a tribe. Jung wrote again that "a tribe's mythology is its living religion, whose loss is always and everywhere, even among the civilized, a moral catastrophe."[20] It is like the state of a living man who has already lost his soul. Such a community has a "faith" that is just outward form, and an experience that is mere sentimentality rather than the *numinosum* of divine revelation.[21]

If "God" is a primordial experience of man, it is the task of individuals, and perhaps whole communities, to express this and other archetypes in the language of myth and ritual. I think a similar task devolves upon those who would deny any real foundation for the archetypal experience. In the tribes of North America we find one of the highest levels of that expression—what Jung calls the great treasures of a thing that provides him with a source of life, meaning and beauty.[22] Alexander claims for Indians a place in the history of mythology comparable to the highest in ancient civilizations.[23] He wrote reverently about all those rituals that include every noble form of religious expression. But rather than merely summarizing Alexander, I might be of more service here to recount my own still very limited experience, mostly among the Northern Arapaho people—experience which has led me now to realize how far we late-arriving Americans have strayed from our origins, experience which now makes me believe that Indian

---

20. C. G. Jung, **Psychological Reflections**, trans. and ed. Jolande Jacobi (New York: Harper and Row, 1961 Torchbook ed.), p, 314.
21. Ibid. p. 313.
22. Ibid., p. 315.
23. Cf. Alexander, **The World's Rim**, pp. xv-xx.

religion could be an expression of that counter-consciousness whose creativity could promise to help restore Spirit to contemporary society. Most of what is narrated is gleaned from the records of Dorsey and Kroeber, or from the family traditions handed on by Bill and Tom Shakespeare,[24] or from conversations and personal witness. I have personally seen how the deepest feelings find expression as I watch vitality and excitement come to the face of an elderly Arapaho as he discusses the meaning of symbolic actions and rituals.

The full tribal myth has rarely been told to outsiders; this is the sacred trust of the Keeper of the Pipe. But we do have partial stories about basic human mysteries. For example, origins: a "man" (not an ordinary man, but perhaps the primordial tribal hero) wanders weeping upon a watery chaos, looking for earth upon which to rest his sacred pipe. His cries are heard by all sorts of animals who come swimming to his aid. They dive for mud, which the turtle finally brings to the surface, and with that bit of earth the man becomes the Creator or Fashioner, covering over the deep with sod, to make an earth upon which all kinds of creatures may live. He completes his work with the molding of a man and a woman, and breathes upon them to make them live.[25]

Or take the concept of God: His presence is not obvious at creation, as it is in Genesis. He is more the High God, but still not the *deus otiosus* of African belief—the deity who once dwelt among men but who has been driven afar off in disgust at man's wickedness. For the Arapaho and most plains Indians, He has a name like Father-Above, far off but interested, listening to prayers and accepting vows, perhaps incarnate in an apotheosis

---

24. William Shakespeare's lectures on his tribe are as yet unpublished, except for where they emerge in his nephew's book hitherto cited. Copies of Shakespeare's 1969 lectures "The Northern Arapaho" given at Lander, Wyoming, are difficult to find.

25. Cf. Dorsey, Op. Cit., The creation accounts and origin myths, pp. 191-228. See also Dorsey and Alfred L. Kroeber, **Traditions of The Arapaho** (Chicago: Field Columbian Museum Publication 81, Anthropological Series, Vol. V), pp. 1-50.

of the tribal hero. It is He who establishes His people at the center of the earth.[26]

Or consider the feeling for life and death: Amid all his trials, for the Arapaho, life is good. Yet death must come. Why? Because someone beyond recorded time threw a buffalo chip onto the primeval deep and said, "as this chip floats, so let man's life be." But Nihancan, the tribal hero, or in some stories an old woman, hurled a rock into the same chaos and it sank. "Rather, thus shall man's life be," it is decreed.[27] In a Blackfoot myth, we find out why: the earth must not become overloaded. Or more important, says the old woman, it is good for men and women to mourn for their loved ones. Bereavement borne well is one of man's noblest opportunities.[28]

But hope is expressed in many ways too. There is to be a reincarnation for man, the Arapaho believe, not as in Hindu tradition because of a weight of evil, but simply because God will let man enjoy several chances at the life he loves.[29] And finally there is to be an ultimate conclusion. The Arapaho tribal fetish is the Sacred Pipe, which is treated with the utmost reverence, for it was with the Creator in His wanderings over the primeval waters, and for it (is it the tribe?) He made earth. Few persons ever see it, but those who do say that it is clogged and unusable, as man's sins have brought about. But the final hope lies in gazing reverently on this pipe, and for this eternal life may be granted.[30] In the present order of time, there is also a gradual petrifaction of the Pipe, and Indian leaders tell me that at the full transformation of the Pipe to stone, the world as we know it will come to an end. Will men be ready when this occurs? Modern Indian writers en-

---

26. Cf. the accounts given in footnote 25 and Starkloff, **Op. Cit.** pp. 325-328.

27. Dorsey and Kroeber, op. cit., p. 17.

28. There are many variations on this myth of "the fall." Cf. Dorsey and Kroeber, op. cit., pp. 81-82.

29. Tom Shakespeare, op. cit., p. 48.

30. Cf. John G. Carter, "The Northern Arapaho Flat Pipe and The Ceremony of Covering The Pipe," **Bureau of American Ethnology Anthropological Papers, No. 2,** Bulletin 119, p. 76.

courage the Indian race to see itself once more as the people chosen to suffer, to bring all men to unity before the end comes.[31] In this combination of ancient myth and modern thinking lies the germ of an Indian theology of hope similar to what Cone, Washington and Roberts have done in the Black community. But if the religious experience of persons who have stood out as prophets and religious leaders is an individuating phenomenon, its effect on the community is even more impressive. If individual transcendence not only divinizes but humanizes, so too does the common experience of the tribe, and it is to the tribe that we now turn.

INDIAN RELIGION AND MAN IN COMMUNITY

Let me quote Wach once more:

> It is significant that the loftiest and most comprehensive concepts of community, those of a universal character, have been possible only through the widening and deepening of religious experience, much as the secularization of these ideas and ideals may have obscured the story of their emergence and evolution to modern man.[32]

From the indicative mood of religious experience there grows the imperative of morality: "become what you already are." For example, St. Paul believed that what *I am* is a new creature living in a new aeon. To find a real relationship to the Holy is a redemptive experience, and from this encounter there emerges what James called a shifting of the emotional center towards harmonious and loving affections.[33] In Indian religion, we witness a partnership between sacred and profane, or better, we realize that nothing created is really profane. The tribe itself, as we have seen, is from the Creator's hands, and has its cohesiveness from recognizing this truth. I have elsewhere pointed out

---

31. Cf. William Willoya and Vinson Brown, **Warriors of The Rainbow,** (Healdsburg, Calif.: The Naturegraph Press Co., 1962), pp. 62-80.

32. Op. cit., p. 377.

33. William James, **The Varieties of Religious Experience,** (New York: Mentor Books, 1958), p. 217.

that a simple tribal sense is not always necessarily redemptive, as we know too well from our own experience! Pressure from the tribe can crush an individual and break his spirit, and since the Holy in itself does not dictate moral values *ipso facto,* monstrosities can be perpetrated in its name. But it is remarkable how, at least among tribes with which I am more familiar, so healthy a sense of community can be found woven into tribal ritual. Such a radication in transcendence seems to produce an ethical tradition worthy of admiration by all societies, to the point where we might as well look into the value of a post-Secular-City "making-holy" of desacralized nature, albeit with cautious discernment! As examples of such a value system, I will propose the practice of giving, tribal welfare, and solidarity in suffering; then the idea of a religiously sanctioned life-cycle, a sense of tradition, the value of play, and poetic expression.

It has become fairly well-known how far apart are the tradition of American frontier of ideas of property and those of Indian culture. Many examples of this can be found in Deloria's book, *Custer Died For Your Sins,* and as the collection of essays, *The Indian in American History* so well illustrates, the placing of blame and the finding of solutions cannot be approached simplistically. But let's take a look at the Indian side. Among the Arapaho, the social sense is even now very impressive. As Kroeber observed in 1907,[34] gift-giving, especially during religious ceremonies, is elaborate and whole-hearted—perhaps at times ostentatious—but always done as a profession of friendship. I have been told many times about this generosity both given and expected, and have experienced it in the form of gifts that might have otherwise brought a good price on the tourist jewelry market. Reciprocity is more or less expected, though not on a *quid pro quo* basis, since services are also a part of gift-giving. The most touching form of this sharing is the practice of a host or hostess

34. Alfred L. Kroeber, **The Arapaho, Part IV: Religion** (New York: Bulletin of The American Museum of Natural History, Vol. XVIII, 1907), p. 18.

at a meal. Guests are expected to bring bags or utensils with them, as I learned too late at my first dinner. This is not merely the frugality of people tried by hunger and want. I was told, "Father, you *have* to take something home, so people there can have part of our feast!" To this same effect, beautiful quilts consecrated to the Sacred Pipe by individual givers are later given to needy persons for practical use. It was not surprising to me that a recent transferral of Kansas property by my own Jesuit superiors back to the Prairie Band Potawotomie Tribe was completed around the altar in a combined Catholic-Indian religious ceremony and accompanied also by a communal feast—though something more than a mere gift was involved here.

Somewhat more subtle are the effects of myth and ritual on the attitude toward birth, growth, maturity, aging and death. As in most cultures, we see here a wide panorama of religious ceremonies celebrating man's life-progress from the Creator back to Him. Once again we find detailed commentary on this in Alexander's *The World's Rim,* where he describes a ritual cycle bearing great similarity to the Hindu approach to life-stages. The significant idea here is the mythologizing of life's passage, again acknowledging its sacredness at every moment. For greater detail, you can consult Alexander's description of the Four-Hills tradition of the Omaha tribe, which I will briefly discuss.[35]

Rites of initiation for infants are common among the tribes, if not universal. Some are being restored. The child in some tribes is presented to the world by the priest in a religious ceremony. Other rites involved naming and ear-piercing, and names given meant something corresponding to reality for the tribe and the individual. By the time of the Arapaho Sun Dance of 1902 in Oklahoma, Dorsey could report only a symbolic presentation of children without ear-piercing.[36] The direct descendent of this Sun Dance, now celebrated by the Wyoming Arapaho, has no formal dedication of children. Sadly, the Christian baptism is generally

---

35. Alexander, op. cit., pp. 170-197.
36. Dorsey, op. cit., p. 179.

too haphazard and offhand to replace such a loss. Even confirmation, which comes later, is alien to the Indian way of doing things. It is ironic how easily these rites of initiation could be reintegrated and incorporated into tribal ritual.

What Alexander describes as the Second Hill is the most sorely missed ritual among today's Indians—the rite of growth. Generally this was a solitary wilderness fast of three or four days, spent in prayer and a vision-quest "for a mystic communion with the powers that shape his world."[37] Alexander notes that the first vigil, which could occur anywhere between eight and seventeen years, was meant to be the beginning of a visionary life that would be profoundly influential on his active career. Thus the vision of the nine-year-old Black Elk, which revealed to him his future vocation to be spiritual leader of his downcast people. As an old man, Black Elk could say,

> I am sure now that I was then too young to understand it all, and that I only felt it. It was the pictures I remembered and the words that went with them; for nothing I have ever seen with my eyes was so clear and bright as what my vision showed me; and no words that I have ever heard with my ears were like the words I heard. I did not have to remember these things; they have remembered themselves all these years. It was as I grew older that the meanings came clearer and clearer out of the pictures and words; and even now I know that more was shown to me than I can tell.[38]

What is also striking is the sensitivity to this vision of the medicine man, Whirlwind Chaser:

> Your boy is sitting in a sacred manner. I do not know what it is, but there is something special for him to do, for just as I came in I could see a power like a light all through his body.[39]

I am reminded here of Schleiermacher's philosophy of childhood religious development, in which the spontaneity of children, not

---

37. Alexander, op. cit., p. 182.
38. Black Elk, op. cit., p. 49.
39. Ibid.

yet ready for verbal argument, is to be respected and encouraged. Tribal stories and teachings among Indians foster this growth, without tending to stifle it with premature and overly cerebral catechetical strictures. I need not enter into this problem here, nor do I find it pleasant to do so, especially since I hope that religious educators now appreciate these subtleties more readily. It is enough to recall the words of Indian parents whose children and adolescents I taught some twelve years ago. Recently I have been advised by them, without any bitterness, how we religious educators could so much more effectively have taught Christianity to Indian children without destroying the spontaneity of Indian language and culture. I receive some consolation now from seeing Indian children leading liturgical prayers in sign language, and even more from the growing tendency of youthful Indians to participate in the fast and prayer of the Offerings Lodge. I pray that it is not a frantic grasp at a last floating straw on the part of all of us—white and Indian alike.

Following the ritual of the mystery of birth and growth, Alexander describes the Third Hill of maturity, and its myth for the passage through the crisis of middle life. As a hunter, a man learned to reverence all life to take only what he needed, because the Powers themselves control a man even as he controls lower forms of nature; life is within a hierarchy. Alexander wrote,

> If, to be a man, the hunter must take life, yet it is with a deeply underlying sense that all life is sacramental, and a sharing, not to be maintained or destroyed at man's lordly whim, but only to be held for an allotted span of petition and proof.[40]

So it was with that great source of middle-life anxiety, the accumulation of property—for the Indian never an end in itself but a commodity to be used for tribal welfare. What was important here was that goods were to be used, or at least saved for communal use, rather than hoarded as capital wealth. Such an outlook has by no means died out among Indians, who still operate

---

40. Alexander, op. cit., p. 184.

on the principle of common usage. Conflicts with white culture
are evident here, as Deloria describes in an incident of the mission-
ary who was indignant that Indians so share goods as to prevent
the emergence of a substantial middle class, which alone can
survive in modern America.[41] I was close to the very incident
that Deloria laments, and would now have to add my own em-
barrassed affirmation to his insistence that Church ideas of
"giving" and "welfare" will have to model themselves on existing
Indian behavioral patterns. How much of this kind of culture
can survive today is perhaps a moot point; how much of it we
whites should be open to is more important. The values of Indians
are much closer to the surface, and yet more spiritually profound:
wealth is always a means to growth, and finally to wisdom. This is
the case with all physical prowess.

There are various societies, what Dorsey called "lodges" among
the Arapaho, through which members learn and exercise wisdom
and gain experience.[42] In our time of anti-war sentiment, many
would see the Indian's ritualizing of military daring as something
to be forgotten. I would be inclined to agree with this, although
most American Indian warfare seems to have been by nature
disinclined to even approach the carnage of a My Lai or a Bang-
ladesh. I would also note that the virtues inculcated by the rituals
of warfare and hunt, such as suspension by rawhide thongs, endurance of thirst and the like, point to qualities that one might need
in many situations—valor, self-assurance, contempt for death. It is
possible to see how this could be a context for the training of
the non-violent militancy of a King or a Chavez.

A moment ago I mentioned "lodges" and "societies" as aids
in living the life-cycle. In Indian tradition, and especially in the
Arapaho culture, where some lodges still survive, there is a profound value to be deduced, and it may be even more important
than the youth rituals. I refer to the problem of aging. It is now

---

41. Vine Deloria, **Custer Died For Your Sins** (New York: The Macmillan Co., 1969), pp. 121-122.
42. Dorsey, op. cit., passim.

clear to me why we in our culture do not understand old age
as a time of realization, and because of their great poverty and
cultural decadence the Indians are falling into the same trap.
The problem is that there is no longer anything that we understand as a wisdom-tradition, nothing requiring a balance between
growth and conservatism, no qualities stored up in the years of
service to ritual and practical experience, for which elders can be
respected. Indians still hold dearly to their independence in old
age however. I know an elderly Arapaho woman who for some
time was placed in a very modern home for the aged, but she
stayed only a few months. She finally insisted on returning to her
two-room tarpaper house on the reservation to live out her days
with some tribal financial support. She had to end her life on
the land, where she could still sit to watch a pow wow or chant
at the Sun Dance. Fortunately, the agent in charge of the matter
was an Arapaho who fully understood her aspiration.

Traditionally, the peak of one's life, in Indian religious societies,
is arrived at in an old age blessed by long experience. In the
1902 Sun Dance we note generally the old age of all the important
figures, and the documented rituals reveal the apologetic nature
of the prayers of a younger participant, who feels called upon
to explain his youth to Father-Above.[43] It is encouraging still
to see elderly persons respected as special functionaries in Indian
social and religious rites. One might notice a "grandfather"
(generally beyond middle age) standing alongside a younger Offerings Lodge worshipper, supporting the man's failing arms during
the dance to the rising sun. This older man is completing his
Fourth Hill; he is coming to the end of the complete cycle. He
ideally enjoys a time of meditation, perhaps of poetry and a simple
looking at nature, and certainly of perceptive wisdom. It is a
time when the spirit balances between worlds, worlds whose
difference is not so sharp as it is for us, realizing that man's
position in life is at best precarious, and that the spirit world
is always right at hand. Alexander describes it:

---

43. Ibid., p. 90.

Life and death are not separate but confluent in Indian lore; and it may be for the very reason that the old man has traversed the ascents of life, and now has mastered the meanings of joy and sorrow, that he is felt also to have a clearer insight into the land of the dead which he is nearing, and is consequently conversant with spiritual meanings.[44]

Death comes, and Indians grieve for the departed as ceremoniously as any other people; their funerals and wakes are a ritualized death therapy. But let us take note of how Deloria rebukes Christian missionaries who try to admonish Indians not to weep for their dead, who are now "better off." Indians need no tutoring about the spirit world, and they need none about how to mourn for their dead either. Perhaps the impressive round dance ceremony in honor of the departed, in which the family leads others in a solemn circle round and round the pow wow circle, bearing a picture of the dead and dancing slowly to the solemn drum beat, is a vestige of the attitude of the Fourth Hill. Indian tradition articulates for us the myth of death in a most unaffected way, and I certainly prefer this, along with our own Christian death rites, to the search for the immortality pill now in vogue. You may recall from comparative religions that the calm acceptance of death belonged to the noble philosophical phase of Chinese Taoism, and the search for the elixer of physical immortality to its period of corruption. My own most vivid memory of a man standing atop his Fourth Hill comes from a visit just a year ago with the holy man of the Northern Arapaho tribe. He very unaffectively gave me a testimony that I sorely wish could be like the history of all Christian missions to the Indians: "I've been a Catholic all my life and I've gone the Indian way all my life. I keep on being a Catholic and going the Indian way, till they come for me—and then I go away."

Too little space remains to go at great length into other aspects of Indian religion and human life, like its superb poetry, but one can read translations of this now in a number of anthologies.

---

44. Alexander, op. cit., p. 196.

However, it is worth noting how a tradition of play and humor intertwines with ritual, as Black Elk describes it in his two testimonies, *Black Elk Speaks* and *The Sacred Pipe*. The old prophet praises the Heyoka ceremony of tomfoolery in which everyone does things backwards—bodies half-painted, heads half-shaved, horses half-decorated, crooked arrows and bows too long to use. Clowning is the order of service. Why is it considered a religious ceremony? Let Black Elk speak:

> You have noticed that the truth comes into this world with two faces. One is sad with suffering, and the other laughs; but it is the same face, laughing or weeping. When People are already in despair, maybe the laughing face is better for them; and when they feel too good and are too sure of being safe, maybe the weeping face is better for them to see. And so I think that is what the heyoka ceremony is for.[45]

There are many other Indian customs in which individuals gifted with visions must go contrary to all natural religious promptings, jesting at suffering, clowning, even laughing at sacred things, saying the opposite of what one means. Clearly, Indians felt that the ludicrous in life is important enough to be given religious sanction, or better, that the storm of boundary situations can often be ridden out on a plank of humor. I have experienced enough Indian humor, being the butt of it at times, to appreciate its power. The stereotype of the dull, humorless Indian (I am thinking now of Boris Karloff in a recent late show rerun of Gary Cooper's old turkey "The Unconquered") is as criminal as that of the unfeeling wooden Indian image. My own experiences would lose in the telling, I fear, so I would rather refer you to Alfred Kroeber's record of Arapaho fables, myths and legends, many of which make Aesop seem quite prim and dour. It is interesting to note that the central comic "trickster" figure of these accounts, both religious and "profane," Nih'an̄can̄ by name, is also the tribal hero like the Algonquian Manito, and finally receives veneration

---

45. Black Elk, op. cit., p. 196.

as Creator, and may even be linguistically the source of the Arapaho name for God.[46] The manner of recording these stories casts an even more humorous light on white America. In the slag-end Victorian era of these works of Kroeber and his mentor George Dorsey, these anthropologists were obliged to take all Arapaho stories with an earthy tint (there are certainly enough of these) and render them in Latin, lest, I presume, uneducated souls be corrupted by their bawdiness. I am grateful for this, thanks to my excess of classical training. In English the stories are funny, and no doubt to a better trained ear than mine they are funny in Arapaho. But in Latin they are side-splitting.

But I am happy to acknowledge that Vine Deloria has also anticipated my thoughts about Indian humor in his first popular book.[47] His examples are entertaining, even for whites who can roll with the punches. But the rationale he gives sheds further light on our discussion: humor is to laugh at oneself and others, thus holding all aspects of life together without letting any one of them drive us to extremes. If such humor can find a home in religious ritual, a person will learn that even his "religion" (I use the word as a Barthian now) is not to be taken with absolute seriousness. Only God receives this worship, and He too lets himself be kidded.

Certainly such is what Harvey Cox had in mind when he wrote *Feast of Fools,* his supplement, we might call it, to *The Secular City,* in which he professes man's need to balance his stern, serious, secular and moralistic ethic with "times" of fantasy. There must be significant *times* or *kairoi* in life—a life so otherwise enslaved to the passage of the sun, the hands of the clock, or the pages of the calendar. Religious festival provides such "significant times," to the point in Indian culture that it still clashes with our clock-directed society in the person of the Indian who lives according to a tribal time-sense but punches a white employer's time clock. This problem must await another time, but

---

46. Cf. Starkloff, op. cit., p. 324, and references indicated.
47. Deloria, op. cit., p. 146 ff.

I cannot resist posing the question, based on a passing comment I heard Michael Harrington make in a recent lecture. If we should somehow succeed in creating extended or even almost total leisure from "jobs" for all people, how important will *chrones* be then? What about *kairos*? Perhaps the ancient will once again have to be acknowledged as an essential part of our permanently "primitive" endowment.

5   Japanese Religiosity and the Humanizing of Man

JOSEPH J. SPAE

I should like to start with a story known to millions of Japanese, the story of Shoma:

> Shoma was born from a poor family. He was stubborn and ignorant but wholly without the usual worldly desires. He never married and, looking at the world differently from others, he spent his entire life wandering east and west, causing people to become more aware of their salvation. His way of enlightening others was simplicity itself. Just by being himself, Shoma caused everyone to appreciate the mercy of Amida.

We find here, in existential terms, all the elements that make for religious greatness, for true humanity: in this story there is timelessness, mysteriousness, freedom, togetherness and humor. There is here, in compact form, what Confucians call humaneness (*jin*); Buddhists, compassion (*jihi*); and Shintoists, sincerity (*makoto*).

It does not matter that we know next to nothing about Shoma except that he was a follower of the Pure Land Sect, born in the province of Sanuki about the year 1800. He was a simple devotee of Amida who bowed to a sleeping dog because "Amida also embraces that beast in his Original Vow." Shoma is a symbol; he is an ideal. In all his ignorance and simplicity he defied the feudal system of his time. He still commands respect, more than a hundred years after his death. His name is mentioned in countless sermons to men and women searching for the wisdom of life.

Shoma is a parable of the power of religion which transforms and humanizes. Shoma is a happy man because he is a good man. He is man fully alive because he is detached from self, present to others and trusting in the basic goodness of things.

I should like to trace the spiritual ancestry of Shoma to the religious currents of Japan or rather to that integrated religiosity which characterizes her people. Much of what I say applies to China (or at least to the peasant China which I knew before World War II), to India, and to other countries of the East. My exposé will be topical rather than logical—which is the Japanese way of looking for truth and inspiration. It will treat of people rather than of books, of religious sentiments rather than of religious systems.

JAPANESE RELIGIOSITY ON THE IMAGE OF MAN

Obviously there are methodological problems underlying this research. I assume that, although the holy is said to be beyond man's direct grasp, this does not preclude the possibility that human systems and secular values *can* also be "religious," particularly when these systems, institutions, and customs are directly seen as "absolutes" even though they may not be "the Absolute," let alone the personal absolute which is God. To be "religious" it is necessary and sufficient that these systems and values be co-determining factors influencing man's destiny and felt by him to be beyond his direct, volitional control. What is "beyond man" is here the equivalent of the holy and the divine (or the imitation thereof, which is the diabolic). Christians would authenticate the "religious" value of systems and action by their fruits: to the extent that they humanize man, i.e. that they make him more attentive to what is good, truthful, beautiful and just; to that extent, Christians would say with St. Ambrose, "by whomever these things are said or done, they come from the Holy Spirit." Man's yearning for and practice of the transcendentals to which I referred is best illustrated by a comparative look at three aspects of religious anthropology: (1) the nature of man, (2) man in relation to others, and (3) man's basic attributes.

(1) *The nature of man*

The word "nature" is derived from a root which literally means "birth" and "growth," the Latin *nasci,* the Greek *phuesthai.*

It designates the individual being in its reality or in its becoming as well as the totality of all being, i.e. the ontological ultimate reality. This concept, in Hellenistic thinking, was never quite liberated from its pantheistic background. It is also, as we shall see, a moral concept.

Man, through self-awareness and freedom, determines the reality which he becomes. By the same token he finds himself also in dialectical opposition with "nature" or natural essences which assume a permanent and predetermined character. Man's existence is basically self-production, self-surpassing, self-transcendence. This transcendental thrust in man is rooted in his being a person, i.e. someone living in an inter-personal dimension, seen as history, society or culture, and—Christians believe—related to an "unconditioned," transcendental Being, manifested to man in truth, goodness and beauty. Man's openness to the beyond-himself is the point of insertion of "the supernatural." While theology holds that man has a supernatural destiny, philosophy sees him as identical with his culture. The above is, in broad strokes, a definition of man's nature derived from existential authors, particularly from Heidegger and Rahner. It lends itself easily to comparisons with traditional Japanese thought.

"Nature" or "*sei*" is a term which should be examined in some detail in relation to the Confucian tradition. It refers not so much to a philosophical as to a psychological and to a moral entity. *Sei* is used for human nature as well as for the nature of animals and things. It also stands for life in general, for bodily organs, and for sex, the agency through which human life is transmitted. Although all men have the same nature and hence are "all equally men" (*Rongo,* 17:2), man's nature may yet come to vary according to whether he pursues or neglects the moral principles upon which his nature is built. This nature, then, is identified with natural feelings, with civilized manners, and with that totality of man's constitution which we call his character.

Another meaning of the Japanese concept of "nature" is "beings in general." In this sense, "nature" is not an object, distinguished from and opposed to man. Rather, man lives in it and is submerged in it through an astonishing emotional and ontological empathy. There is an irresistible tendency to personify or rather to anthropomorphize the concept of nature. In practice, any effort which tends to overcome the tension between subject and object, i.e., between man and his environment, is seen as an act of virtue which contributes to man's happiness because it is basically true to the demands of his nature.

The tendency not to differentiate between subject and object accounts not only for the basic immanental character of Japanese religiosity but also for a remarkable openness to the numinous and for frequent, almost compulsive, recourse to the irrational and the non-scientific as a shortcut to suprasensorial reality. In other words, the theory of religious projection which is predicted upon the distinction between subject and object (thereby tending to weaken the value of subjective experience as a legitimate source of information on the religious nature of man) has been kept in check by Japan's religious traditions, particularly by Zen. This means that, basically, the Japanese refuse to proclaim the "death of God" in the name of science. They are not inclined to accept the monopoly of science or of rational thinking as the sole and absolute source of religious information. Academic circles in Japan may have heard of Freud, Marx and Jung, the three great names behind the theory of religious projection who see religion mainly as an answer to man's needs. But their influence has not penetrated to the heart of Japanese religiosity, as witness the success of the new religious movements in Japan.

Man's nature is linked to man's becoming. The Japanese insight, while accepting a certain fixity and continuity in human nature, strongly favors the point of view that man grows, as life goes on, toward his final maturity, expressed in Shinto harmony and in Buddhist salvation. Human history is not dependent on cosmological causes or cyclical events as some Chinese Confucianists have taught. Man, or rather man-in-society, is master of his destiny.

There is no generally accepted theory on man's origin, and no idea of creation. Not much is said about the hereafter. There is no metaphysical *Angst* about heaven or hell. Salvation is definitely on earth; the quest for it is pragmatic and utilitarian. No doubt, all the above statements require qualifications. But I believe them to be generally true.

(2) *Man in relation to others*

The Japanese live in the present; and they live, as the literal translation of the word for "human being," *ningen,* indicates, "among men." This insertion in society, by which is meant the family and the country as well as the neighborhood and the circle of friends, is traditionally more emphasized than the assertion of individuality, although the pendulum is obviously swinging at present in the opposite direction. Such a situation, as we shall see later, when examined in the light of recent psychological and theological thought, leads to interesting conclusions regarding the role of the Christian presence in Japan.

The human community extends beyond that of the living. One gains the impression that the personality range of the Japanese is double: it is both individual and corporate. Ancestors function as the subconscious personification of tradition. In this sense, they, too, are members of the corporate personality. In the totality of experience, the security of being attuned to the corporate personality is often more compelling than a search for individual experience. Consequently, deviant conduct is ethically suspect. The Japanese type of emotional compenetration between man as the microcosm and nature as the macrocosm is well known. In all strains of Japanese thought, this macrocosm tends to become a mystical entity. "Nature" is then held up as the model of man's perfection. Its imitation is the hallmark of virtue.

Although the Japanese word for nature, *shizen,* does not have at first glance the meaning of "order" and "adornment" which is that of the Greek word *"cosmos,"* it nevertheless conveys a strong impression that being is "of-itself-as-must-be" (*onozukara shikari*), by which is meant that everything has a place in the world wisely provided for it. Against this *providentia rerum* man dares not revolt without impunity. Rather, he must endeavor to be "from-within-himself" (*onozukara*) what he is or should be (*shikari*). Only at this interior height does man reach perfection. While there has been considerably less philosophizing in Japan than in

China where attention centered on the *status* of man in his world, or in India where man's ultimate *goal* became the focus of religious thought, the Japanese inherited from both these countries a man-centered orientation to which they added their own twist of practicality. Buddhism notwithstanding, the Japanese never shared with the people of India a negative attitude toward the world of things. They show little metaphysical concern for man's significance or value in the cosmic setting. Utterances such as that of Sophocles to the effect that "there are many marvellous things, but none more marvellous than man" are, to my knowledge, only obliquely found in Japanese literature.

It is understandable then why the Japanese traditionally pay little attention to an "ultimate" beyond human society. They are not "being grasped" (as Tillich would say) by the problem of man's relation to God, although there are, at least in Shinto, explicit references with the *kami*. There is, indeed, a measure of transcendence deep at the heart of Japanese life. The Japanese are familiar with fear and awe and wonderment before the mystery of existence.

(3) *Man's basic attributes*

Western philosophical thought generally defines the *person* as the actual and unique reality of a spiritual being. This reality is incommunicable; it belongs to itself and is its own end. The human person is finite because individualized in matter; he is also infinite because he craves totality and universality. At death his spirit is set free to reach an untrammelled, divine-like life. To these elements of Platonic-Aristotelian philosophy, Jewish-Christian thought added new elements such as God's call to man for partnership, for co-responsibility and co-creativity. Later, through this haze of philosophical concepts pierces the light of Christian faith. With this light comes a novel awareness which bids man reassess himself. The Greek metaphysics of being is replaced by the experience of man's historicity and finality. Man is a being who is loved by an infinite being; he is both subsistent in himself (that which modern philosophy calls in-sistence), and open to the other (what is called ek-sistence).

Many of the above elements which stand out in the Christian tradition with particular sharpness can also be found in Japanese thought. An analysis of the notion of person will show that, in Japan, attention goes preferably to his activities rather than to his substance. In other words, attention is directed toward his ek-sistence rather than to his in-sistence; it puts man within nature, not over nature. Japanese thought does not see him primarily as a cog in the universe (the Greek concept), nor as a partner of God (the Christian idea), but as essentially a social being with a spark of the divine (the Confucian human nature, *sei,* is endowed by heaven), destined for a life of happiness through communication with the *kami* (the Shinto heaven) and yearning for deliverance from change and suffering (the Buddhist nirvana and paradise or *gokuraku*).

The dichotomy between body and soul has never been a problem with the Japanese as it was with the Greeks. On both sides it is assumed that man is a compound of spirit and matter with no definite boundary between them. But, in Japan, body and soul are not seen as two poles, inevitably in a state of tension. Far less is the body seen as the source of man's sinfulness. In Buddhism it is the mind which plays that role; in Shinto, the distinction is all but unknown, and the source of evil is found outside rather than within man. Whatever the merits of the Japanese position, the popular approach to the human admixture is not philosophical but practical. Except in scholastic Buddhist thought there is no problem of corporality, and no strife of flesh versus spirit. Emphasis remains on the psychosomatic unity of man and on his wholeness through integration of all faculties. The goal is happiness, perceived as a balanced hedonism which offsets reason with emotion. All this amounts to a formula of life, ideally found in an exercise of freedom and authenticity. It is precisely this formula which stamps Japanese thought concerning man with an earthy and a "Japanese" flavor.

JAPANESE RELIGIOSITY AS A HUMANIZING EXPERIENCE

Every true religious experience is an echo of the divine in man.

The sacred and the divine are manifest in nature. In a country of stunning natural beauty, Japanese religious feeling has, from ancient times and up to the present, been singularly at home in a cosmic dimension. Religious observances take place in shrines and temples which architecturally, one would almost say, emotionally, blend into the surrounding nature. The whole setting is felt to be an integral part of a cult sacralizing the ideal interpersonal relationship expressed in the Shinto word *shinjin-waraku,* the harmony between gods and man. I tend to think that it is precisely this cosmic, and hence, exterior, dimension of Japanese religiosity which has basically resisted the tendency toward total interiorization typical of the Buddhist concept of life, a tendency also known to Western spirituality, particularly since the end of the Middle Ages. Nevertheless, if association with the visible world counteracts the interiorization of religious sentiments, it also collaterally promotes their communal manifestation, a fact which may be illustrated by the Japanese bias for *matsuri* or group celebrations versus private and individual religious practices.

The Japanese religious feeling is cosmomorphic, rather than anthropomorphic, which is merely another way of saying that it is a primitive or archaic experience. Not only has it preserved a strong awareness of the symbolic power of the natural elements but it also shows all the characteristics of "participation." By this is meant that the Japanese remain deeply conscious of taking their place in the unfolding of a global mystery. This "participation" explains many facets of their religious psyche, in particular the role which Shinto *kami* and Buddhist *hotoke* play, not only in Japanese popular worship, but in many facets of family and national life. This natural insertion of "the divine" in Japanese society underlies the fact that a symbolic and religious meaning is attached to the world of man. In the line of a positive religious evolution, such a meaning would point to three ascending stages: (1) from an original, cosmomorphic stage of Japan's religious feeling, through (2) an intermediary, anthropomorphic stage, toward (3) its final development (one suspects under Christian influences), a theomorphic perception of man and the universe.

There is another aspect of primitive religiosity found in the

Japanese consciousness. It consists in a subconscious tendency not to distinguish between the subjective and the objective, between self-experience and other-experience, between feeling and knowledge. The consequences of this national state of mind for Japan's religious experience are many. There is no accurate separation between man's three distinct faculties as seen by Western philosophy; reason, will and feeling. In the West, reasoning or knowledge is the principal means of acquiring truth. This may also be so in Japan but it does not seem to apply to the religious sphere. Religious truth is primarily seen as the result of feeling, that diffused, unarticulated feeling which is expressed by the word *kimochi*. This anti-intellectual vein of Japan's religious mind has fostered a lack of attention to historic accuracy or, in other words, it has in extreme cases contributed to an equal valuation of reality and fiction. Whatever can be visualized, or even strongly desired, is often thought to be real, obtainable, and even already obtained. This presupposes that thoughts and words are as potent as actions. The hard facts of life may contradict this stand which, in final analysis, is a form of magic. But it remains true that for the believer, facts, fiction and feeling are complementary and co-active, and that religious experience can be gained by each one of them. Basically, they are seen as the triple source of knowledge. In religion, "the heart is more important than the head" (*risei yori kokoro*). This "feeling" for religious values as elements of poise and integration is uncommonly strong in Japan. It is a measure of the humanizing influence which religiosity exercises upon her people.

RELIGIOSITY AND HUMANIZATION: THE EXISTENTIAL DIMENSION

The pursuit of the *humanior* emerges on many facets of Japanese national life. From these facets I shall only select two: estheticism and intuition, and I shall connect them with those religious values of which they are the radiant garb.

(1) *Estheticism and the fuller life*

Rabindranath Tagore has said that Japan's unique *dharma* is her esthetics. *"Dharma"* is a way of life; it is either religion or a substitute for religion. Tagore's insight is confirmed by Professor Kishimoto Hideo: "In their achievements religious values and esthetic values are not two different things. Ultimately, they are one for the Japanese." Kishimoto finds the reason for this fact in the basic empirical nature of Japanese culture. Religion, particularly Buddhism, instructs man how to reach a tranquil mind. Only in this state of tranquility—or of religion—can the artist work. Art and religion have the same goal; hence, religious and esthetic values are one. The same is said in other words by the former president of Tokyo Gakugei University, Masaaki Kōsaka who maintains: "Beauty is not limited to physical beauty, i.e. beautiful flowers, beautiful women, but involves spiritual beauty also. Therefore, Japanese ethics demands purity of mind, refinement of tastes, harmony of individuals, mutual love." Hajime Nakamura has often stressed the primacy of the esthetic, the intuitive and the emotional in Japanese culture.

At this point I should like to enter two caveats. The first one is this: the insistence on estheticism as one of Japan's principal national attitudes ought not be exaggerated. Japan has an abundance of artistic achievements to its credit. But there is no lack of ugliness and vulgarity, particularly in those departments of life where the traditional ways do not apply. The second caveat is this: the Japanese, unlike the Indians, never displayed an intensive search for God-realization through esthetic cultivation. Their enjoyment of the beautiful is real and deep but it does not lift them much higher than the clouds which veil Fuji's splendor; it entails no metaphysical *Angst;* it remains very much of this world. If, consequently, Japanese estheticism is identifiable as religion, this religion will rarely be one of ultimate commitment.

I feel that D. T. Suzuki, the great Zen scholar, comes near the truth when he states: "The esthetical appreciation of nature always involves something religious." And by "religious" he means being "super-worldly," going beyond the world of relativity where we are bound to encounter oppositions and limitations. "Estheticism now merges with religion," Suzuki concludes. This "merger" is by no means always smooth or acceptable by Christian standards. It is only too evident that the center of Japanese estheticism is not necessarily outside the world. "Beauty is a fearful and a terrible thing," said Dmitri Karamazov. It may tempt man to *hubris,* the idolatrous effort to capture the divine within the human. The Japanese recognize themselves in the portrait of Natasya Fillipovna in *The Idiot.* Her beauty was too much for her. "That dazzling beauty was quite unbearable . . . such beauty is power. . . . With such beauty one can turn the world upside down." Like Natasya, they live under the category of perfection. And in their lives, many values seem to be strained to perfection.

What is the relationship between estheticism and religion in Japan? The traditional religions of Japan, and even more so, their modern offspring have intuitively accentuated the nexus between art and religion. Their concern is man's mental state, his peace of mind. Balance and tranquility of emotions rather than behavioral patterns (as would be stressed by the Christian commandments) are their prescription for happiness. Hence, esthetic sensibility reflects man's original goodness, they feel, and thereby becomes the hallmark of moral perfection. The artist is a good man; the good man is an artist. Religion and art are one.

Evidently, the statement that "religion and art are one" is only true in the Japanese context which sharply distinguishes between religion as doctrine and religion as ethic. It is only in the latter sense that the dictum applies. Japanese religiousness takes for granted that to the inwardness of the esthetic perception corresponds an outwardness which is its ethical reflection. In this sense, the Japanese hold that subjectivity of feeling connects with objectivity of deed. This intrinsic connection is acutely perceived as an ethic dimension which is the ascertainable touchstone of spiritual authenticity. Incidentally, the technical expression of this behavioral correspondence between intention and act is *shinjō wo tsukusu,* which, literally translated, means "to *exert* fully one's *true feelings.*" We have here a perfect case of the Japanese triunity which encompasses action, thought and emotion. The adjectival forms which express this perfectly integrated state of mind are preferably taken from the vocabulary of art. He who, in trying circumstances, is consequential with his deepest feelings is said to be "a beautiful person," *utsukushii hito*. In illustration of what I mean, this case: I have known a young man who wished to know how it felt to die while listening to Beethoven's Fifth Symphony and leaped from the top of Himeji Castle into the moat below along which an orchestra was playing his favorite composition. The papers related that the young man (who explained his motives in a note) "died beautifully," *kirei ni shinda*. To Japanese observers suchlike deeds imply a definite moral purity and sincerity, pregnantly expressed in that "amuletic word" *makoto*. Might we not render that word, I ask, by "conscientiousness"—and draw the theological conclusions?

If the Christian reader should wish to pause at this point and reserve judgment, I shall understand. No doubt he wonders about the moral value of that "purity" to which I have referred. The answer to this question does not come easily, so varied and intimate are the factors involved. Yet, this "purity of intention," and this "conscientiousness" are of the greatest importance to our thesis that, in Japanese perspective, esthetics may have considerable redemptive value—also from the Christian point of view.

Let me say this much in explanation. "Purity" is selflessness (*muga*) and dispassion (*muyoku*). Its attributes are awareness (*kakugo*) and determination (*kakushin*). Its fruits are truth (*shin*), goodness (*zen*), and esthetic pleasure (*bi*). Impurity, on the other hand, is attachment (*shūchaku*) with its consequences, the whole catalogue of sins.

Esthetic activities (and Japanese life is replete with them) are exteriorizing channels for, or restraining agents of, man's basic sentiments such as love, anger, fear. To be an element of satisfaction to the self and others, these activities—and the management of these sentiments—require a definite asceticism or discipline of mind and body, in other words, a type of *zen* or *yoga*. Such an asceticism draws the heart away from gross material and sensual pursuits. It graces the turbulent and troubled mind with emotional equanimity and mental calm (*seijaku*). Art is such a discipline; hence, art is a form of asceticism (*gyō*).

All this may sound strange to Western ears which have never been attuned to Confucian music as a call to virtue, nor felt entranced by Shinto dancing as an expression of cosmic harmony, nor meditated to the lilting rhythm of Buddhist psalmody as a murmur of selflessness. It is, indeed, difficult for the West to realize that Confucian humaneness (*jin*) is the substratum of peace of mind, that Shinto purity (*seimei*) means cheerfulness, and that Buddhist compassion (*jihi*) is the source of high esthetic joy.

(2) *Intuition and the interior life*

There is a legitimate place for intuition in ethics and religion, a fact which is implicitly recognized by all spiritual currents in Japan. I have tried to prove that, in Japan, intuition is supplemented by reasoning and cannot be pronounced infallible. The Japanese will less frequently decide to do a thing "because it is good" than because "it has to be done." To them, the "ought" is the "good." The Japanese believe, perhaps with greater assurance than Westerners, that they readily "feel" what they ought to do by intuition. Actually, this intuition is the terminus of a process of reasoning, explicit or implicit, which takes into account the immediate consequences of an action. If there is anything "Japanese" in this procedure, it might be found in its speed and immediacy, in one word, in its spontaneity. This "spontaneity" (a word which could be adequately translated by *chokkansei*) rests upon an intuitive knowing of man by man. As Nyozekan Hasegawa has correctly seen, it is essentially an ethical bearing which exteriorizes itself not only in certain attitudes, gestures and words, but even in the clothes we wear, in the utensils we use in the atmosphere in which we live. Such "spontaneity" is a kind of pre-understanding, a pre-ontological knowledge. It is a whispering spirit in the heart of the hearer which allows him to grasp intuitively—and often correctly—the individual totality of the situation. But it must not be forgotten—and the Japanese also instinctively feel this fact—that this pre-understanding requires an *intellectual sympathy* in the Bergsonian sense through which one is transported into the interior of a person or a situation to merge with what is unique and consequently ineffable therein. And it is at this point that intuition connects with ethics and religion.

The Japanese are strongly aware of the fact that man's fundamental choice in feeling-with-the-other and understanding him cannot be made on the basis of general principles alone. It must be understood and decided within the empirical situation, i.e., by means of experience. No matter what one's definition of "experience" is, there is always need for time and reflection before one can enter into the most intimate being of another and merge with it. This indicates that the "immediacy" and the "speed" to which I have referred, have definite limits and that knowledge of persons and situations is indispensable to determine the moral direction of one's life. Ethics and religion are never based on intuition alone.

All men, and all religions, have their privileged moments of spiritual experience. Such moments are marked by a profound intuition of truth and love. In their basic thrust, such moments leave behind all historical conceptualizations which so easily diversify and disunite. They are a grace and a *kairos* we all need.

The Japanese feel that there is also an intimate connection between intuition and the nature of truth. The combined influences of early Japanese thought, as manifested in the *Manyoshu,* and in Buddhism have contributed to the strong conviction that truth belongs as much to the ethic as to the noetic order; and that nothing is really true until it is also proven to be good. It is at this point that intuition—which, as we have seen, is a guide to action—plays an important role. The very relative concept which the Japanese have of verbal truths and their strong conviction that "sincerity" (*makoto*) is the standard to which, in its noblest expression, truth must conform—all this proves that truth "must be done." Such is also the biblical view on truth. The Japanese *shinjitsu* comes near to the Hebrew *'emeth*. It entails the inner perception that, what one affirms and sets out to do, is true because it is good, and good because it is true. Truth is a kind of certitude and confirmation (*kakushin*) that one is doing what one ought to do. The Japanese feeling for truth is, thanks to its very intuitiveness, dear to Christians for whom truth and goodness are based upon "the grace to feel in the innermost part of our being God's will for us."

Estheticism and intuition as elements of the religious expe-

rience are correctives to the over-conceptualization of religion.
They remind us of a fact which Otto has stressed throughout his
The Idea of the Holy, namely, that what is most distinctive in
religion cannot be put into words. This is the "non-rational" part
of religion, the part which cannot be conceptualized. This part
which Otto calls "the numinous experience" is based on feeling
and on consciousness.

In comparison with the thrust of Japanese religiosity, Christianity is a religion of which an important part is put into "words."
Such a thrust corresponds to the Greek-Roman genius which
nurtured the Christian formulation of faith. The "non-rational"
element in Christianity, for all that, was not forgotten: it leaps
forth from the interior awareness of Christian believers and reaches
its peak in their mystics.

To be understood by Japan, Christians must stress that there
is much in their religion that cannot be put into words, and that
"rationality" is not enough for a lover of Christ. They will meet
at this point the innate awareness of the Japanese that, at the core
of all serious religion, there is an element of "non-sense," something, that is, which cannot be perceived by the senses and which
is not verifiable by the scientific mind. This "non-sense" is not
nonsense. It is, in fact, the only thing that makes sense—to
intuition.

TWO JAPANESE LITERARY GENIUSES AND THE HUMANIZING OF MAN

I should like to add to the classic religious traditions of Japan,
which so far received attention, a word about the latecomer which
is Christianity, and illustrate what happens when two of Japan's
great cultural and religious men are intimately confronted with
the message of the gospel.

My first example is Ryūnosuke Akutagawa (1892-1927)
and his parable *The Death of a Christian*. The scene of the
parable is the church of Santa Lucia in Nagasaki. A young boy
is found exhausted at the entrance and cared for by the Bateren
(Fathers). They love him for his piety, his sweet countenance,
and for his voice, pure as that of a girl. About the time Lorenzo

(for that was the name they gave him) comes of age, the rumor spreads that the daughter of an old parasol-maker in the neighborhood—also a Christian—has fallen in love with him. Questioned, Lorenzo denies the fact. Somewhat later, a love letter from the girl is found in the convent garden. "I never talked with her," Lorenzo maintains. Time passes. One day, the girl confesses that she is pregnant with Lorenzo's child. Lorenzo is expelled from the community, and reduced to beggary. In due time a girl is born to the parasol-maker's daughter.

Fire breaks out in Nagasaki and the parasol-maker's house is enveloped in flames. Only Lorenzo dares to rush in and save the baby. From the billowing fire he emerges, his clothes aflame, and thrusts the unhurt child into its mother's arms. As he collapses, crushed by burning timbers, the young mother kneels before a priest, confessing: "This baby girl is not the child of Lorenzo. . . . I loved Lorenzo. But he, having deep faith in God, did not return my love. Hence I started hating him and lied about the father of the child. Yet his noble mind refused to scorn me for my sin. He risked his life to rescue my baby from the inferno of the flames. For his mercy and his solicitude, I adore him as Jesus Christ come back to earth." "Martyr, martyr," cries the crowd as Lorenzo breathed his last. Only then, his burnt and torn clothing revealed that Lorenzo was—a girl. Akutagawa concludes his story with this compelling paragraph:

> Nothing else is known of the life of this girl. What does it matter anyhow? Life's sublimity is gauged at the high peaks of inspiration. Man makes life worth living when, from life's dark sea of cares, he tosses aloft high up to the stars a wave which mirrors in its crystal foam the face of the moon about to rise. Therefore, are not those who know Lorenzo's last, the very ones who thereby know all her life?

This parable illustrates the magic touch of Christianity which changes whatever passes through its heart. The sinning girl is Japan. The boy—or rather, the boy who really was a girl—is Christianity, because love and loyalty, sacrifice and hidden passion —all these, in Japan, are symbolized by womanhood. A mystic attraction goes out from this spirituality and grips the imagination of Japan. There is a hidden, jealous, nagging, despairing love which lurks in Japan's feeling toward Christ and his ideals. Clearly, that love is vague, unspoken, untutored, erratic and confused. But it is there, very deeply felt; and it brings forth, as we have seen, the most surprising reaction.

Akutagawa, so Japanese and yet so haunted by Christ, was a highstrung man whose nerves were far too brittle for his genius. He contemplated death for years and slowly, deliberately, he rose up to that "highpeak of inspiration" by which he wanted to be judged. The end came when he was thirty-five, and after he had written magnificently on all the noble suicides of East and West, as well as on Christ, who died unequalled in suffering, graciousness and love. He drank poison. When they found him dead on the morning of July 24, 1927, there was an open Bible at his side. I do not know on which page of the Bible Akutagawa held his hand in death. My guess is that it was on the page of the Beatitudes. For this is where Japan's thirst for goodness, truth and beauty encounters "Christ come back to earth." In this encounter there is no destruction of whatever lives with the Life; there is only transformation on the Way to the Truth.

My second example is Endō Shūsaku, famous author of *Silence* (tr. by William Johnston), the piognant story of a priest who apostatized. Those of us who have met Endō, who saw him frequently on TV, who listened to him at meetings and in the circle of his friends, know that he is perpetually wrestling with one single theme: his personal confrontation with Christ. The "Japanese" in him squirms in an ill-fitting European suit from London's Saville Row. It was this European suit which "my mother pulled over my head at age twelve; the sleeves are too short and the pants are too long. This suit is my Christianity." All this goes to say that *Silence* is largely autobiographical, and that, in part, the priest and the apostate stand for Endō. Shall they apostatize? Shall he shed his ill-fitting Western clothes? "I could not if I wished," he answers in a recent book of literary self-criticism, *Ishi no koe* ("Voices of Stones," Tokyo: Tojusha, 1970). "I simply haven't anything to put on instead; I still love my mother; I feel to the marrow of my bones the strength of Christianity."

Endō is fascinated with Christ. Of the many Christian authors in Japan, he is the only one who lives with every breath what Dibelius once expressed as "the most terrible thing that can happen to man: to meet Christ, to look him in the eye, and to fall in love with him." Endō's Christianity cramps his literary style. "I go through agonies," he confesses, "when I think how my readers, who hardly know anything about Christianity, shall interpret what I write." He feels underprivileged compared to Julian Green who could describe, in *Moira,* "a snow-covered night" and be reasonably sure that his readers would find, in the snow, the double meaning of God's grace and man's purification. But Endō does not have this privilege. His literary expression of Christianity cannot be two-dimensional; rather, he fears, it is as flat and unimaginative as the untutored mind of his readers. Hence his impatience at not being understood when he writes these simple and yet tragic words in *Silence*: "The priest placed his foot on the *fumie.* Dawn broke. And far in the distance the cock crew." Who, in Japan, knows that it is Peter's story all over again?

And yet Endō has to tell the Japanese of his love; of his fascination with Christ. He explores every avenue of encounter, even apostasy—for love of neighbor, which is Christ. He might go as far as Ryunosuke Akutagawa, that literary genius of the twenties with whom he has so much in common. Like Akutagawa, Endō is haunted by Christ. I would not be surprised if, like Akutagawa, he should have thought of "that highpeak of inspiration" which is death in imitation of all the noble suicides of East and West. I hope, of course, that Endō won't drink poison as did Akutagawa in the night of July 24, 1927. But I wouldn't be surprised if he did because he simply couldn't wait any longer to meet Christ. And I feel pretty sure that, if he did, he too would hold his hand on an open Bible so that, in death, he can quote the Beatitudes to the angels. . . .

Endō manfully tries to have his readers struck by the presence of Christ. He often refers to "a dog" and "a bird." For him, the eye of a dog and of the bird is the eye of Christ. This is the eye which stares at them from the *fumie,* the copper image of the

Lord which apostates must trample. The novelist, Endō says, remorselessly portrays living man. Hence he thrusts his hands in the dirtiest and darkest of man's pockets. This may sit ill with a certain type of Christian literature. But any other approach would be a betrayal of God's grace; it would be ramming God's salvation down men's throats. And to this, with reason, both God and man would object. Endō knows that true religion evokes clear resonances. When he writes he is bewitched with a face mirrored in his heart, the face of Christ. There is the eye of Christ which lovingly, compassionately and yet so quietly, looks at man. When this eye wanders off, then the novel slips into irrelevant psychological reporting; it loses touch with supreme reality, that inner judgment before which no falsehood lifts its head.

What then is salvation? It is not for man to judge. No one should judge the apostate, except "the eye." The tragic tensions between culture and faith, love and hatred, loyalty and betrayal, all these are understandable enough. But there is always "the eye." The eye *is* judgment. The eye is final. The eye is love.

Indeed, whilst the cock crew, dawn was breaking.

As I pointed out, the methodology followed here concentrates on some religious ideas and beliefs of today's Japan. I assumed that these traditions and beliefs have a "religious" meaning when, in the final instance, they manifest man's conscious effort to give himself, to find himself, and to transcend himself. I am aware that, like any other people, the Japanese intimately feel at the high moments of their religious experience that such matters as death, man's expectations in regard to the hereafter, his efforts to penetrate the riddle of uncontrollable suffering, frustrations, and many similar vital questions have a definite bearing upon their identity, goal-setting and capacity for happiness, now and later. Somehow, I submit, many Japanese are also conscious of the fact that such matters transcend the empirical world in which they move. They feel the need to seek light and strength in faith; they turn to a vaguely perceived spiritual power; they turn, in a word, to the supernatural and the transcendental. I assume that every act which has a humanizing influence also participates in the sacralization or hominization of man and, consequently, becomes part and parcel of his religious life. From a theological point of view, I further assume that revealed and unrevealed truths are often coterminous and complementary, and that they live harmoniously together—be it in however rudimentary a fashion—in the hearts of many Japanese.

A BIBLIOGRAPHICAL NOTE

Detailed source material related to this article will be found in four volumes by this author: **Christian Corridors to Japan** (2nd rev. ed., 1967); **Christianity Encounters Japan** (1968); **Japanese Religiosity** (1971); **Shinto Man** (1972); all published by and available at the Oriens institute for Religious Research, Chitose P.O. Box 14, Tokyo 156, Japan.

6   The Continuing Challenge of Existentialism

David H. Hopper

Not long ago Benjamin DeMott, a professor of English at Amherst, described the growing popular usage of the word "existential":

> "A foreign entry, heavy, hard to pronounce, fast in the forties, faded in the fifties, the word looked a foot too long. . . . Despite the handicaps, though, 'existential' is breaking through. Improving its place steadily, unfazed by cheapening, inflation or technical correction, it's closing once again on high fashion."[1]

The term receives currency in educational reform, in the theater, in women's liberation, in "Black theology," in the definition of the counter-culture. However, the sense, or meaning, of the word can generally be determined only in its particular context. At times "existential" is used synonymously for "good," "real," "exciting," "authentic," and a number of other emotive adjectives. Especially common is its usage in connection with the experience of "immediacy," the "now" as opposed to the anticipation of the future or perspective upon the past. Thus, Norman Mailer, in speaking of the Columbia University student strike, asserted that the strike was ". . . existential because these kids went out and did something that they had never done before, and they did not know how it was going to turn out." And DeMott quotes another student spokesman as saying: ". . . the trick is not to know what's going to happen next, that's existential, that's being."[2]

---

1. Benjamin DeMott, "How Existential Can You Get" **New York Times Magazine** (March 23, 1969), p. 4.
2. Ibid.

These patterns of usage and thought certainly suggest a continuing vogue for the term "existential" and also for at least some aspects of the existentialist point-of-view. But if one notes this popular and—one must say—superficial acceptance of existentialism on the one hand, it is necessary also to take account of the studied rejection of existentialism on the other.

For example, it is not without reason that the spokesmen for revolutionary action have found only a strange and temporary ally in the existentialist point-of-view. The reshaping and liberation of the individual through some pattern of social engineering and revolutionary restructuring of society is simply not a postulate of existentialist thought, despite the efforts of Sartre and Merleau-Ponty to work out some positive relationships with progressive, revolutionary movements. Books like Erich Fromm's *Socialist Humanism*[3] and George Novak's *Existentialism Versus Marxism*[4] make it abundantly clear that the committed, socialist revolutionaries are extremely dubious about the individualistic and "non-scientific" starting point in most existentialist thought. And they properly perceive, I believe, the optional nature of the existentialist social ethic. Thus Milan Prucha argues against existentialism that

> "the existential structure of man as an objective being and as a being whose essence is **not inherent in the abstract individual but is of a social nature** has always determined the most general features of the mode of man's self-assertion.... By abolishing exploitation, by overcoming the division of labor, ... through the development of scientific knowledge, ... by the creation of a new type of social relationship, etc., the individual can gain new possibilities for liberating himself from his egocentric self-isolation and for participating in the being of all mankind."[5]

And George Lukacs writes against Sartre that

---

3. Erich Fromm (ed.), **Socialist Humanism: An International Symposium** (New York: Doubleday and Co., 1966).

4. George Novak (ed.), **Existentialism Versus Marxism: Conflicting Views on Humanism** (New York: Dell Publishing Co., 1966).

5. Fromm, op. cit., pp. 160-61.

"In his (Sartre's) popular pamphlet he says, 'Nothing can be good for us which is not good for everyone,' and in another place: 'At the same time that I will my own freedom it is my duty to will the freedom of others. I cannot set my own freedom as goal unless I also set that of others as my goal.' This sounds very fine. But in Sartre it is only an electric insertion into Existentialism of the moral principles of the Enlightenment and the Kantian philosophy."[6]

Parallel to this Marxist rejection of existentialism is the drift away from existentialist perceptions that is traceable in a movement such as the Students for a Democratic Society. The SDS initially drew a great deal of its inspiration from the thought of Albert Camus,[7] but as the SDS moved from a position of opposition to the established order toward an outline of a future program it found fewer and fewer nurturing resources in the thought of Camus.[8] Since Camus rejected hope in the future as a valid source of human meaning and demanded the lucid acceptance of meaninglessness (or the "absurd") as the basic human condition, one could, as an individual, rebel against meaninglessness; but this possibility did not offer a solid basis for a social program.

These elements of existentialist thought—and the kind of opposition and rejection that come from futuristic and society-oriented movements—have tended to diminish the role of the existentialist perspective in the patterns of intellectual construction that are part of our current scene. Theodore Roszak's *The Making of a Counter-Culture*[9] is another instructive example of this phenomenon. Roszak makes favorable use of the word "existential" but seems studiously to avoid any reckoning with the major content of existentialist thought. One is probably safe in assuming,

---

6. Novak, op. cit., pp. 149-50. Cf. also p. 44.

7. Although Camus and Sartre held differing existentialist views, their common starting point in the isolated and alienated individual posed similar difficulties in constructing a social program.

8. Martin Marty and Dean Peerman (eds.), **New Theology No. 5** (London: Macmillan Co., 1968), p. 41.

9. T. Roszak, **The Making of a Counter-Culture** (New York: Doubleday Co., 1969).

however, that he regards it as another human, reflexive rejection of technocratic society, an argument similar in a way to the Marxist assessment of existentialism as a dying spasm of the bourgeois era. As a position distinct from Marxism however, Roszak's romantic project is likely to encounter existentialist opposition especially in its mystical, shamanistic propensities.

If one moves from the realm of secular thought to that of theology—and here I must make it clear that I speak primarily of Protestant theology because of greater familiarity with that sphere, one notes a similar tendency to reject the existentialist position. The key figure in the most recent theological rejection of existentialism—though little, or no, discussion of this has taken place— is, I believe, Dietrich Bonhoeffer the martyr, Bonhoeffer the political activist, that has seemingly afforded relief from the heavy and lugubrious atmosphere of the theological struggle against liberal optimism, natural theology and National Socialism. It really required one who had lived that struggle to open the doors to new, more romantic, theological statements of Christian faith. And it is this that I take to be the dominant pattern over the last ten years of Protestant theological discussion. Bonhoeffer, to my mind, represents a theological equivalent to John Kennedy on the American political scene. Kennedy, the man of vigor, the war hero, the aristocrat, breathed a new, romantic, idealistic spirit into American national life, a spirit left a-borning by his tragic assassination. Unlike Kennedy's, however, Bonhoeffer's death reinforced and greatly furthered his influence.

Bonhoeffer's theological impact was, of course, the result not only of the life he lived and the death he died; it was due also to the theological visions he conjured from his prison cell. His vision of "man come of age," his hopes for a "religionless Christianity," his idealization of the secular man, his insistence that man be addressed at the point of his strength rather than his weakness: these elements in Bonhoeffer's prison letters opened up vistas of "freedom" and "light" for many in the theological world. And the exploration of these new realms of Christian thought represents the pattern, I think, of most Protestant theology and of a fair amount of Catholic thought as well.

It is to be noted that in Bonhoeffer's prison letters all is not vision and spiritual venturing. There are also the bold negations. And chief among these is his attack upon existentialism—and what he took to be its twin, psychotherapy. Bonhoeffer writes:

"We have, of course, the secularized off-shoots of Christian theology, the existentialist philosophers and the psychotherapists, who demonstrate to secure, contented, happy mankind that it is really unhappy and desperate, and merely unwilling to realize that it is in severe straits it knows nothing at all about, from which only they can rescue it. Wherever there is health, strength, security, simplicity, they spy luscious fruit to gnaw at or to lay their pernicious eggs in. They make it their object first of all to drive men to inward despair, and then it is all theirs. That is secularized methodism. And whom does it touch? A small number of intellectuals, of degenerates, of people who regard themselves as the most important thing in the world and hence like looking after themselves. The ordinary man who spends his everyday life at work, and with his family, and of course with all kinds of hobbies and other interests too, is not affected. He has neither time nor inclination for thinking about his intellectual despair and regarding his modest share of happiness as a trial, a trouble or a disaster."[10]

Other statements attacking existentialism in this vein are to be found in Bonhoeffer's prison letters. And, even though they lack a judicious grasp of the nature of existentialism and obviously failed to anticipate the wide appeal of existentialism in the late 1940's and 1950's, they seem to have been given a great deal of weight by many who, during the 1960's sought to develop the theological hints and suggestions of these prison notes.

Certainly William Hamilton, one of the leading spirits in the short-lived "Death of God" movement, makes clear his debt to Bonhoeffer,[11] though he does not dwell at length on a rejection of existentialism. Harvey Cox, in his attacks upon existentialism, does not make explicit reference to Bonhoeffer; but he *does* declare his major debt to him.[12] In *The Secular City* Cox manifests a

---

10. Dietrich Bonhoeffer, **Letters and Papers from Prison** (New York: Macmillan Co., 1962); p. 196.

11. T. J. J. Altizer and W. Hamilton, **Radical Theology and the Death of God** (Indianapolis: Bobbs-Merrill Co., 1966); p. 52.

12. Daniel Callahan (ed.), **The Secular City Debate** (New York: Macmillan Co., 1966); pp. 205-14.

puzzling contradiction in his appraisal of existentialism—a fact
perhaps most charitably explained as the result of journalistic
urgency. On the one hand, he hails Camus as a prime example
of profanity,[13] a positive attribute in Cox's sketch of the secular
man; and, on the other hand, he intersperses his overall discussion
with captious and summary dismissals of the existentialist point-
of-view.[14]

What is evidenced in these positions of Bonhoeffer, Hamilton,
and Cox is a reading of history which enables one to anticipate
the future and, in the process, to write off existentialism as a
temporary, historical aberration. The situation in regard to Jürgen
Moltmann's *Theology of Hope* is not greatly different. Moltmann's
attack upon existentialism is, on the surface, more studied; but
it is clear that the logic which demands its rejection is equivalent
to that of the Marxists and other historical futurists. A close
student not only of Bonhoeffer but of the "revisionist Marxist"
Ernst Bloch, Moltmann's criticism, though at a few points thought-
provoking, tends to indulge in ridicule and concludes with the
facile consignment of existentialism to a well-defined—and ma-
ligned—historical niche. He asserts:

> "The despairing surrender of hope does not even need to have a
> desperate appearance. It can also be the mere tacit absence of meaning,
> prospects, future and purpose. It can wear the face of smiling resig-
> nation: **bonjour tristesse!** ... **Of all the attitudes produced by the
> decay of a non-eschatological, bourgeois Christianity, and then conse-
> quently found in a no longer Christian world,** there is hardly any which
> is so general as **acedia, tristesse,** the cultivation and dandling manipu-
> lation of faded hopes. But where hope does not find its way to the
> source of new, unknown possibilities, there the trifling, ironical play
> with the existing possibilities ends in boredom, or in **outbreaks of
> absurdity.**"[15]

Tempting as it is to want to take time to exegete the quoted passage

---

13. Harvey Cox, **The Secular City** (New York: Macmillan Co., 1965);
pp. 70-78.

14. Ibid., pp. 68-69, 79-81, 251-53.

15. J. Moltmann, **Theology of Hope** (New York: Harper & Row, 1967);
p. 24. Italics mine.

and to point up the lack of reason which at points pervades its argument, let us instead treat the matter of Moltmann's interpretation of the historical incidence of existentialism and begin to state the major thesis of this paper: the need for theology to recognize in existentialism a provocative and long-term alternative to Christian faith.[16]

The Marxists, the romantic counter culturists, the secular theologians, the theologians of hope: all tend to use a similar argument against existentialism, that is: that existentialism is a limited, passing, historical phenomenon which is usually best understood as a symptom of cultural sickness. Thus, Pyama Gaidenko, a Communist spokeswoman, asserts; "Existentialism brings into the open the question of the crisis of bourgeois culture."[17] Roger Garaudy, the French Marxist, describes existentialism as "metaphysical pathology."[18] Harvey Cox declares that "existentialist theologies and philosophies do not partake of the spirit of the emerging age but symbolize rather the passing of the old."[19] "Existentialism," Cox argues, "appeared just as the Western metaphysical tradition, whose social base was dismantled by revolution and technology, reached its end phase. It is the last child of a cultural epoch, born in its mother's senility."[20] And Moltmann, in the passage quoted above, speaks of existentialist attitudes born of "the decay of a non-eschatological, bourgeois Christianity."

The effort of these critics to consign existential to a dying culture, to write it off as a phase of the historical process, is, I think, too convenient and unconvincing a means of getting rid of a troublesome protagonist. And thus I would like to suggest that although there has been special currency to the existentialist

---

16. In speaking of "existentialism" here I recognize the fact that in popular usage what is most often referred to as "existentialism" is the non-theistic existentialism of Heidegger, Sartre, Camus.
17. Novak, op. cit., p. 275.
18. Ibid., p. 156.
19. Cox, op. cit., p. 80.
20. Ibid., p. 252.

point-of-view in the twentieth century world—a matter which I also want to treat, the roots of existentialism reach back into antiquity and the kinds of questions it addresses itself to are, in fact, enduring questions.

In support of this thesis one can, of course, cite Paul Tillich, who, in his classic treatise, *The Courage to Be,* attempts to dissect the nature of human anxiety and argues for its threefold character in relation to death, guilt, and meaninglessness. He asserts that "in all three forms anxiety is existential in the sense that it belongs to existence as such and not to an abnormal state of mind as in neurotic (and psychotic) anxiety."[21] In short, and against many present day critics, Tillich argues that the concerns of existentialism are *not* those of a sick mind or a dying culture, but are grounded in the very nature of the human experience. Tillich further suggests that over the long course of Western history it is possible to discern periods in which the different forms of human anxiety have played dominant spiritual roles. He notes:

> "The distinction of the three types of anxiety is supported by the history of Western civilization. We find that at the end of ancient civilization ontic anxiety (death) is predominant, at the end of the Middle Ages moral anxiety (guilt), and at the end of the modern period spiritual anxiety (meaninglessness). But in spite of the predominance of one type the others are also present and effective."[22]

It is true that some support is given here to the idea that anxiety manifestations occur at the *end* of major historical periods, but the total argument and the range of historical vision strongly counter the summary dismissals of existentialism. What is of note and what carries weight at this point is the thoroughness and probity of Tillich's inquiry. For one who was deeply imbued with a love both of philosophy and history and who in his younger days also entertained great enthusiasm for historico-cultural turning

---

21. Paul Tillich, **The Courage to Be** (London: Nisbet & Co., 1952) pp. 38-39.
22. Ibid., p. 53. Words in parentheses added.

points (the *kairos* doctrine), Tillich, in *The Courage to Be,* manifests a perspective upon history and human life which compels thought and sober judgments, judgments that stand out starkly against Harvey Cox's glib assertion: "There is something immature about existentialism."[23]

Any serious consideration of the existentialist literature must, I think, take account of the appeal to the traditions of Antiquity that are found in that literature. This appeal both to Greek and Hebraic sources is neither forced nor formal but stems from the supposition of a shared human experience. It suggests a measure of stability in man's experience of life that defies the contemporary confidence in impending breakthroughs into new levels of consciousness. Rudolf Bultmann, a representative of existentialist theology, remarks:

> "It is often said that mythology is a primitive science, the intention of which is to explain phenomena and incidents which are strange, curious, surprising, or frightening, by attributing them to supernatural causes, to gods or to demons. . . . But there is more than this in mythology. . . . Myths express the knowledge that man is not master of the world and of his life, that the world within which he lives is full of riddles and mysteries and that human life is also full of riddles and mysteries. Mythology expresses a certain understanding of human existence. . . ."[24]

And Bultmann concludes that this understanding of human existence is *not* to be easily displaced and written off by modern man with all of his boasted competencies.

The experience of death, the mystifying encounter between human consciousness and a world hauntingly strange to that consciousness raised questions, stirred fears, in the mind and heart of ancient man. And can we not honestly say in us as well? Blaise Pascal, neither an ancient nor modern man, spoke of a *human* experience when he said: "I am frightened, and am aston-

---

23. Cox, op. cit., p. 253.
24. Rudolf Bultmann, **Jesus Christ and Mythology** (New York: Scribner's & Sons, 1958); p. 19.

ished at being here rather than there; for there is no reason why here rather than there, why now rather than then. . . ."[25] These evidences suggest a stability, an enduring quality to aspects of human experience which at the very least raise doubts about the potential of history to alter radically the human situation and the most basic human concerns. Paul Roubiczek, the Cambridge philosopher, offers an argument similar to what is being suggested here when, in arguing for a *moral* nature of man, he states:

> "As man develops in an historical way, we find that morality, at first, also develops in accordance with different historical conditions; in early times, in primitive society, it hardly exists in the form in which we have been discussing it. Yet the surprising fact is, not that it develops at first in the same way as everything else but that it suddenly becomes stable whenever and wherever a certain stage of development is reached."[26]

As Roubiczek here asserts the attainment of a moral consciousness in man, I suggest the attainment of an existential consciousness, a consciousness, for example, that allows Greek tragedy to speak to us at the level not only of aesthetics but at the level of personal existence.

There remains, however, a point in the arguments against existentialism which still has to be treated—and that is the matter of the historical incidence of the existential point-of-view. Put another way, the question is: if existentialism is grounded in an enduring human experience, in a deep-seated anxiety and sense of alienation, how does one explain the peculiar outbreak of existentialist thought in the twentieth century? Why is it that only in these latter times has it emerged as a philosophical school of thought?

To answer this question in its entirety would demand more time and space than allowed here, but the main point that I would like to make in response to this question is that while I have argued against an overwhelmingly determinative role for history in the definition of human existence I do not maintain that it plays

25. Quoted by Paul Roubiczek, **Existentialism For and Against** (Cambridge: Cambridge University Press, 1964); p. 57.
26. Ibid., p. 84.

no role at all. I find myself here fairly close to the view of Tillich as set forth in *The Courage to Be,* to wit, that at certain points in history different aspects of the existential experience tend to dominate. I do not myself, however, care to designate these points, or periods, as "the end of ancient civilization" or "the end of the Middle Ages." With Tillich, however, I feel that our present era, perhaps up to most recent times, is deeply troubled by the experience of meaninglessness. This experience is rooted in the frustration of human hope and purpose that is represented in the two world wars that have been fought in this century. The First World War, for the European Continent at least, shattered the illusions of liberal progressivism and produced massive, unanticipated horrors. The same can be said of the Second World War, except for the possibility that it may have represented an even more profound frustration of human purpose in that naiveté and illusion were thought to have been chastened. For such a concerted historical effort and immense sacrifice to pass over into the unexpected and bitter impasse of the Cold War meant nothing less than defeat for the belief in historical purpose. And this, I think, helps to make understandable why reactors to French defeat (Sartre, Camus) found themselves with an audience of world-wide proportions.

To argue in these terms is, I believe, realistically to assess the nature of the existential experience in both its solitary, individualistic character (the encounter with death, self-world alienation) and also in its corporate-historical dimensions. And it suggests an answer to why the ideologists of hope and futurism seem so often driven to exorcize the existentialist spirit with spleen and ridicule. Not only is the individualistic existential point-of-view a threat to utopian social hopes, but the historical existential experience, rejected though it may be by a later romanticism, insinuates into hope the spectre of despair. This, I believe, is why Lukacs says:

> "Taking eternal death as goal makes man's existing social situation a matter of such indifference that it might as well remain capitalistic. The assertion of death as absolute fate and sole destination has the same significance for today's counter-revolution as formerly the con-

solation of the hereafter had. This . . . casts light too on the reason
why the popularity of Existentialism is growing not only among snobs
but also among reactionary writers."[27]

And also Garaudy:

". . . the 'ravages' of Existentialism are very limited: it is not an epi-
demic that can grip a whole nation. This thinking severed from the
real world has no hold on the working class. . . . It involves at most
a titillation or mild fever affecting a few intellectuals who consider
themselves 'demobilized' after the Resistance movement had played
its part. Cut off from the broad masses of the people, they like to make
a god of their confusion and their 'nothingness'; and, believing that
they cannot find a goal worthy of their talents, they are satisfied with
ersatzes and bargain-counter revolutions."[28]

These harsh attacks by the spokesmen of Marxist ideology make
it clear, I think, that however things may be in the theological
world, in the "scientific" world of historical materialism, existentialism represents a disturbing presence. It is a presence that
troubles Marxist theoreticians because they fear that in the face
of a dying ideal, an unrealized hope, the existentialist alternative
will pronounce the words of death. This analysis does not necessarily imply that existentialism essentially nurtures itself upon
faltering hopes; but only that its view of the human reality
Marxists—and of many other futurists as well.

But what then is the meaning of existentialism for theology?
I certainly do *not* propose that theology should take its cues from
the existentialism of Camus and Sartre, but I *do* suggest that
it not be ignored—as I fear it increasingly tends to be in our
present theological situation. I want also to propose that despite
our present turn toward romanticism, atheistic existentialism probably represents the most troubling alternative to Christian as well
as to Marxist faith.

What makes the situation different for theology, however, is
that there is an authentic existentialism that arises on Christian
soil and is clearly not to be subsumed under the cloak of despair

---

27. Novak, op. cit., pp. 146-47.
28. Ibid., p. 163.

and courage. Christian existentialism, however, shares some things with that other existentialism of which we have been chiefly speaking, and I would like to suggest that at one point something of a common word might be spoken. This has to do with history and the overemphasis upon the importance of history in the definition of human existence.

We have heard, and we have heard again, about the importance of history within the Judaeo-Christian tradition. And while not wanting to deny the historical nature of the Exodus, or the Christ event, I do not see that the content of God's revelation in those events necessarily establishes history as such as the special sphere of God's continuing revelation. It may be, of course, merely a reflection of some sort of existentialist prejudice, but it seems to me that the most popular forms of recent theology have generally followed this line. They have moved most powerfully from the base of an interpretation of history to some secondary statement of Christian content, with the result that Christian content tends to be swallowed up by the historical interpretation. Thus with rapid shifts in the course and moods of the historical scene theology becomes increasingly a journalistic enterprise. For example, the optimism and exuberance of the "secular city" followed by a few "hot summers" becomes the dreariness of the "urban problem" which in turn has now been enveloped by "ecological fright." The chief result of all this seems to be that the theological presses continue to hum and thereby prove their "relevance."

Some years ago, in a situation of historical excitement, a theologian who is clearly no longer "relevant" spoke of the Lordship of Christ in the following terms:

"He is indeed with us every day until the end of the world, but not in such a way that He would be swallowed up by our days and the bold grasping which is the significance of our days, not in such a way that we should have the mission and authority to interpret our days as we like, so as then to give His holy name confidently to the thing our interpretation has created."[29]

---

29. Karl Barth, **The German Church Conflict** (Richmond: John Knox Press, 1965) p. 32.

This warning derives from the world of faith and is different from the protest against historism deriving from the ethos of secular existentialism, but the latter protest needs to be heard as well. It is a protest rooted in the individualistic realities of existential alienation, an awareness that reckons with the presence of death and the distance of nature and society, and it asks rhetorically of the future: "to what end?" It understands the life pattern of a man who, when he dies, is remembered for a while by his friends, a while longer by his loved ones—but then they die, and the memory fades and is gone. History and the events of our time have the capacity to stir us, provide us at times with challenge, with occasions for dreaming and daring. But the elderly wise among us may utter Biblical words:

> "There is no remembrance of former things, nor will there be any remembrance of later things yet to happen among those who come after." (Eccles. 1:11)

Besides engendering reserve and caution about what one claims for history, existentialism offers a challenge, I think, to the assumed utility of the concept of secularity. Recent theology has rather deluded itself, I believe, with the thought that the secular world is a nascently Christian world. It can *be that* by the grace of God but hardly by the imaginings of theological poets. However much some Christians may comfort themselves with the thought that Biblical faith may have contributed to the "disenchantment of nature" and the "desacralization of politics," the imagined neutral, secular world is rather illusory. And if it does exist, it is more a home to the existential man of Camus and Sartre than it is to the life of faith. Rudolf Bultmann speaks more perceptively, I believe, when he asserts that "Faith is not flight from the world nor asceticism, but *desecularization* in the sense of a smashing of all human standards and evaluations."[30] This suggests that the idea of the "secular saint" is a false notion—and perhaps

---

30. Rudolf Bultmann, **Theology of the New Testament**, vol. II (New York: Scribner's Sons, 1955); p. 76.

also that of "religionless Christianity" when it is interpreted to mean little more than an embrace of the secular world.

The final point I would like to make in regard to existentialism and its challenge to theology has to do with the spirit in which theology is done. While I agree that the dour theologian is frequently a burden to the Church, I doubt that the frolicsome, blythe spirit is any less a burden. One is struck of late with the presence in most sober Presbyterian churches of airy, colorful banners, generally home-sewn, spelling out "love," "peace," "joy," "good news"—usually with a border of daisies. Now I trust I won't be misunderstood on this. I believe the Gospel *is* "good news," "joy," "peace," "love"—but I don't believe that bannering and wall-painting is somehow going to translate us into that celebrative world envisioned by some. In fact, I sometimes suspect that the emblazoned words are more an expression of our longing than of our faithful (?) human reality.

What existentialism injects into this pattern of possible wishful thinking is the suggestion that every human emotion and longing does not necessarily possess a justifiable ground, that the human animal can very well imagine himself into a world of his own construction and thus fail of an authentic life. Theodore Roszak, for example, enthusiastically proclaims the program of the "counter-culture" in just such wishful terms. He writes:

> "... the task of life is to take this raw material of (man's) total experience—its need for knowledge, for passion, for imaginative exuberance, for moral purity, for fellowship—and to shape it all, as laboriously and as cunningly as a sculptor shapes his stone, into a comprehensive style of life."[31]

At another point Roszak asserts that the counter-culture is demanded by our "unfulfilled psychic needs." Contrary to the supposition of many, it is not existentialism that flees the real world to find solace in unbridled subjectivism. Rather, existentialism calls men to face the realities of self-delusion and the necessity of a searching honesty. A theology that is worth its salt cannot be less.

---

31. Theodore Roszak, op. cit., p. 235.

III

A CHURCH MORE CHRISTIAN:
The Humanization of the People of God From Within

7 Revolution in Catholic Theology

BERNARD J. F. LONERGAN

I may assume, no doubt, that everyone is aware of the profound changes that have occurred in the thought of Catholic theologians during the present century. But to enumerate in detail just what changes have occurred in the thought of individual theologians seemed to me to be just a long litany that presupposed a great deal of not very illuminating research. So I have been led to think it more profitable to inquire into the causes of such change and to estimate which changes have come to stay.

Now it is in the area of scholarship—of the linguist, the exegete, the historian—that the most startling changes have occurred in Catholic theology. More rapidly in the fields of patristic and medieval studies, more slowly in the field of scripture, there gradually have been accepted and put into practice new techniques in investigating the course of history, new procedures in interpreting texts, new and more exacting requirements in the study of languages. The result of these innovations has been to eliminate the old style dogmatic theologian. For the old style dogmatic theologian was expected (1) to qualify his theses by appealing to papal and conciliar documents from any period in Church history and (2) to prove his theses by arguing from the Old Testament and the New, from the Greek, Latin, and Syriac fathers, from the Byzantine and medieval scholastics, and from all the subsequent generations of theologians. But the new techniques in history, the new procedures in interpretation, the new requirements in the study of languages reveal the performance of the old style dogmatic theologian to be simply out of date. For the new techniques, procedures, requirements demand specialization. They demand that opinions be based on full knowledge. They consider it self-evident that one man cannot know all there is to be known either on the

Old Testament or the New, either on the Greek or on the Latin or on the Syriac fathers; and, as the same holds for the Byzantine and the medieval scholastics and for their later successors, the old style dogmatic theologian has simply become obsolete.

There are further and far more general consequences. Culture used to be conceived normatively. It was something that ought to be, and accordingly, *de iure* if not *de facto,* there was just one culture for all mankind. It was the fruit of being brought up in a good home, of studying Latin and Greek at school, of admiring the immortal works of literature and art of the classical period, of adhering to the perennial philosophy, and of finding in one's laws and institutions the deposit of the prudence and the wisdom of mankind. But exploration, anthropology, the proper interpretation of texts, and the composition of critical histories have given currency to an empirical notion of culture. A culture is simply the set of meanings and values that inform the way of life of a community. Cultures can decline rapidly, but they develop only slowly, for development is a matter of coming to understand new meanings and coming to accept higher values. Moreover, any notable culture has a long history: it has borrowed from other cultures; it has adapted what it borrowed into its new context; it has effected the development of its own patrimony. Cultures are many and varied; they all have their good points and their deficiencies; and the ideal culture is far far rarer than the ideal man.

To grasp the empirical notion of culture leads to a grasp of what is meant by a person's historicity. What counts in a person's life is what he does and says and thinks. But all human doing, saying, thinking occurs within the context of a culture and consists in the main in using the culture. But cultures change; they wax and wane; meanings become refined or blunted; value-judgments improve or deteriorate. In brief, cultures have histories. It is the culture as it is historically available that provides the matrix within which persons develop and that supplies the meanings and values that inform their lives. People cannot help being people of their age, and that mark of time upon them is their historicity.

What I have been saying has considerable importance in the

Church's task of preaching the gospel to all nations. A classicist could feel that he conferred a double benefit on those to whom he preached if he not only taught them the gospel but also let them partake in the riches of the one and only culture. But the empirical notion of culture puts an entirely different light on the matter. The preacher's task now becomes one of inserting the gospel within a culture in which it has not been known. To make it known there, there must be found in the local language the potentialities for expressing the gospel message, and it is by developing these potentialities and not by imposing an alien culture that the mission will succeed.

There are further implications to the shift from a normative to an empirical apprehension of culture. For the normative apprehension projects upon laws and institutions a permanence and rigidity that the study of history finds to be illusory. From the normative viewpoint one will think of the Church as a *societas perfecta,* a perfect society endowed with all the powers necessary for its autonomy. From the empirical viewpoint one will conceive the Church, as in the *Handbuch der Pastoraltheologie,* as a *Selbstvollzug,* as an ongoing process of self-realization, as an ongoing process in which the constitutive, the effective, and the cognitive meaning of Christianity is continually realized in ever changing situations.

There are not a few writers who assert that the normative view of culture and the universal uniformity it implies derive from Greek thought and, specifically, from Greek philosophy. And while I believe it is true that the Greek philosophers did not know about the techniques developed by more recent exegetes and historians, it remains that a more exact understanding of the normative approach is to be had by turning from the Greek philosophers to the humanists, the orators, the school-teachers, to the men who simplified and watered down philosophic thought and then peddled it to give the slow-witted an exaggerated opinion of their wisdom and knowledge. After all, from a contemporary viewpoint it seems an incredible conceit to suppose that one's own culture is the one and only uniform and universal culture.

However that may be, we must go on to further sources of

change in the thought of Catholic theologians. Not only is it true that the Greek philosophers did not foresee the implications of contemporary hermeneutics and history. It also is true that they did not grasp contemporary notions of science and of philosophy. Only in the nineteenth century was it recognized that Euclid's *Elements* was not the one and only geometry, but just one out of many possible geometries. Only more recently did mathematicians deduce their conclusions not from necessary truths but from suitable postulates. For years physicists proclaimed the necessary laws of nature, but less than fifty years ago they began to speak of the statistical probabilities of quantum theory. Even economists spoke of the iron laws of economics, only eventually to renounce them and turn their hand to advising bureaucrats on the probable results of this or that course of action. There has emerged a new notion of what a science is, and it in no way corresponds to the knowledge of the cause, knowledge that it is the cause, and knowledge that the effect cannot be other than it is, that is set forth in Aristotle's *Posterior Analytics.*

The content of modern scientific doctrine is not an intelligibility that is necessary but an intelligibility that is (1) possible and (2) probably verified. Moreover, to give an account of a modern science one cannot be content to list logical operations, that is, operations with respect to terms, propositions, and inferences. The modern scientist does perform logical operations: he defines, formulates, infers. But he also observes, discovers, experiments. Moreover, the two sets of operations are interdependent. Discoveries are expressed in definitions and formulations. Inferences from formulations are checked by observations and experiments. Checking by observation and experiment can give rise to new discoveries, and the new discoveries in turn generate new definitions and formulations to make science not an unchanging system but an ever ongoing process.

There is a further departure from Aristotle in modern science. Aristotle wanted the sciences to derive their basic terms from metaphysics. Potency and act, matter and form, substance and accident were key concepts. Such sciences as physics or psychology obtained further key concepts proper to their respective fields by adding appropriate further determinations to the metaphysical basic terms. In contrast, modern science sets up its own basic terms; it does so by deriving them from empirically established laws; and such are the concepts of mass, temperature, the electromagnetic field, the elements of the periodic table, the branching of the evolutionary tree.

Now when the modern procedure is adopted in cognitional psychology, then one's basic terms will refer to conscious operations and one's basic relations will refer to conscious relations between operations. Through such basic terms and relations one can tell just what one is doing when one is coming to know. From such cognitional theory one can go on to explaining why doing that is knowing, and so arrive at an epistemology. From cognitional theory and epistemology one can go on to setting up a metaphysics, that is, to state in general what one knows when one does come to know. On this showing metaphysics ceases to be the first science on which all other depend. But ceasing to be the first science has its advantages, for now a metaphysics can be critically established; every statement it makes about reality can be validated by a corresponding cognitional operation that is verifiable.

We have been observing both in science and philosophy a shift from the intelligibility that is a necessity to the intelligibility that is a possibility and, as well, probably verified. Now this shift means the dethronement of speculative intellect or of pure reason. Neither the scientist nor the philosopher has at his disposal a set of necessary and self-evident truths. He has to observe external nature. He has to attend to his own internal operations and their relations to one another. Neither the observing nor the attending reveal necessity. They merely provide the data in which insight may discern possible relationships, and which further experience may confirm as *de facto* valid.

The dethronement of speculative intellect has been a general trend in modern philosophy. Empirical science led to empiricist philosophy. Empiricist philosophy awoke Kant from his dogmatic slumbers. The German absolute idealists, Fichte, Schelling, Hegel, attempted to restore speculative reason to her throne, but their

success was limited. Kierkegaard took his stand on faith, Schopen-
hauer wrote on the world as will and representation, Newman
toasted conscience, Dilthey wanted a *Lebensphilosophie,* Blondel
wanted a philosophy of action, Ricoeur is busy with a philosophy
of will, and in the same direction tend the pragmatists, the
personalists, the existentialists.

I am far from thinking that this tendency is to be deplored.
What once was named speculative reason today is simply the
operations of the first three levels of consciousness—the operations
of experiencing and inquiring, understanding and formulation,
checking and judging. These operations occur under the rule
and guidance of the fourth level, the level of deliberating, evaluating, deciding. Philosophers and scientists recognize this fact
when they deliberate about the proper method to be followed
in their work.

I have said that contempoary hermeneutics and history have
made the old style dogmatic theologian obsolete. I have gone
on to argue that the contemporary notion of science and its consequences in forming the notion of philosophy are quite different
from the notions entertained up to the eighteenth and nineteenth
centuries. It is not only the old style dogmatic theologian that
is obsolete. It also is true that the old style dogmatic theologian
cannot be replaced on the basis of old style notions of science
and of philosophy.

What the new style is to be, I cannot prophesy. But perhaps
I should mention what I tend to think. First, then, there is going
to be a lot less metaphysics. It has ceased to be the basic and
universal science, the *Grund- und Gesamt-wissenschaft.* General
theological terms will find their roots in cognitional theory.
Specific theological terms will find their roots in religious experience. There will be far less talk about proofs, and there will be
far more about conversion, intellectual conversion, moral conversion, religious conversion. The emphasis will shift from the
levels of experiencing, understanding, and judging, to the level of
deliberating, evaluating, deciding, loving.

In the present century, then, theology is undergoing a profound change. It is comparable in magnitude to the change that

occurred in the Middle Ages, that began with Anselm's speculative thrust, Abelard's hard-headed *Sic et Non,* the Lombard's
Sentences, the technique of the *Quaestio,* and the fusion of these
elements in the ongoing process of Commentaries on the Sentences,
Quaestiones disputatae, and the various *Summae.* Then, without
any explicit advertence to the fact, theology operated on the
basis of a method. For over a century it brought forth precious
fruits. To theology as governed by method and as an ongoing
process the present situation points. If that pointing is accurate
and effective, then the contemporary revolution in theology also
will have the character of a restoration.

**Commentary on
"Revolution in Catholic Theology"**

WILLIAM E. MURNION

As I understand Father Lonergan, he is concerned with indicating the causes and consequences of the revolution (in the sense of "profound change") which, he says, everyone is aware has occurred in Catholic theology in the present century. As he sees it, the development of scholarly specialization (linguistic, exegetical, and historical) has led to the obsolescence of dogmatic theologians; the adoption of a historicist perspective on culture, to the reconceptualization of the Church as a *Selbstvollzug* with the mission of adjusting to the potentialities of each culture; and the critical reconstruction of metaphysics, to the revision of theology as a process of articulating methodically the meaning of religious conversion. He expects this revolution to result in the restoration of theology to the vitality it enjoyed in the Middle Ages.

That is what Father Lonergan says, but is it so? First, has there really been a profound change in Catholic theology in the present century? Not if the professionalization of theologians through functional specialization is supposed to be the main indication. That was just the latest step in the evolution of the role of theologians from priestly caste to clerical state of professional society—in each case an intellectual elite adapting to changing social conditions to maintain its place in the social structure. But while theologians have been saving their lives by changing their skins, there have been two revolutions, which Father Lonergan does not mention, the effect of which has been to make not just dogmatic theologians but all theologians obsolete. The most immediate has been the rejection by Catholic college students of theology as a meaningful part of their education, so that in Catholic colleges today theology survives mainly as a core requirement, and theology departments have had to become departments of religious studies to survive. But the more basic has been the economic, political, social, and cultural revolution of modern times, which has rejected theology as the ideology of the *ancien régime* against which it has directed all its forces. The response to this revolution has come mainly not from professional theologians but from pastors such as Camillo Torres, Dom Helder Camara, the Berrigans, and Bishop Gumbleton, who, divining the Christian inspiration behind modern revolution, have initiated a practical revolution in theology when a theoretical revolution was lacking. Therefore I think that Father Lonergan has been as wrong to assume a profound change within Catholic theology as he has been to ignore the modern revolution without it.

But even if theology has not undergone a change profound enough to correspond to modern revolution, has Father Lonergan been correct in analyzing the cultural impact of this revolution as merely the realization that the West is one among many cultures, with the consequence that the Church has had to reconceive of itself in dynamic and relative terms? Far from it. The shift in perspective which opened the West to the historical and global dimensions of culture has been a conscious and deliberate rejection of the adequacy of the Christian culture of medieval Europe. The religious import of modernization has been secularization—the denial of the validity of the theological perspective traditional in Western culture since its origins in Athens and Jerusalem. It was this perspective that prompted the West, nowhere more than in Rome, to regard its culture as normative, and it has been the rejection of this perspective that has allowed the West, apart from Rome, to consider other cultures as meaningful. The consequence of this shift in perspective has been no mere reconceptualization of the role of the Church but rather the death of God in Western culture. In these circumstances the mission of the Church is not to adjust to other cultures but to realize it is an integral part of Western culture, and the reconceptualization of the Church should be undertaken not in a futile attempt to modernize itself but in a realistic effort to adjust itself to being a medieval carryover. Therefore I think Father Lonergan was engaging in wishful thinking when he depicted the Church as a *Selbstvollzug* with a mission to other cultures.

But even if the Church has become outmoded in modern culture, is Father Lonergan correct in thinking that the effect of modern science *via* metaphysics upon theology will be the reestablishment of religious categories on a sound basis in cognitional method? I doubt it. In the first place, the change from the Aristotelian to the modern conception of science was less a shift from a demand for causal certitude to an acceptance of empirical probability (for Aristotle was well aware of the need for empirical verification in science, and modern science originated from a desire for certitude in empirical knowledge) than a rejection of a theological basis for belief in favor of a human basis, a basis that would justify the mastery and not just the contemplation of nature, that would articulate itself in mathematical postulants and not in metaphysical principles, that would advance toward pragmatic, not speculative goals. The change, therefore, as I see it, has been primarily substantive and only secondarily methodological. Similarly, the effect of the invention of modern science upon philosophy has been only incidentally the reactionary attempt to reconstruct metaphysics on subjective (cognitive, anthropocentric) instead of on objective (essential, cosmocentric) grounds and principally the gradual supplanting of metaphysics with scientific method, formal logic (foundational mathematics), and hermeneutic (positivist, linguistic, phenomenological, historicist, pragmatic, existential, or structural). The consequence has been an efflorescence of the sciences—natural, human, and philosophic —with each grounding itself in the self-critical development of its own appropriate method. Thus the effect of modern philosophy upon theology has not just been the attempt to re-establish classical theology on the basis of transcendental method but even more importantly the displacement of theology by religious studies. This is a field that opened up with the modern assumption of a global and historical perspective on culture, developed apace with the appearance of the human sciences, and began to come into its own with the realization of the need for a method commensurate to its horizon. Like the rest of modern science, religious studies operates without the presupposition of the existence of God, thereby retaining a capacity to evaluate Western culture critically as well as to appreciate other cultures emphatically. Yet since it has developed from a religious perspective, its general categories are religious, its specific categories historical, social, psychological, anthropological, political, phenomenological, and structural. At the same time that theology, the first science ever to emerge, has been atrophying into the ideology of the Church, religious studies has been developing into the science of the ultimate meaning to human existence. I believe Father Lonergan is wrong, therefore, in predicting a restoration of theology on the basis of scientific method.

My differences with Father Lonergan, then, on the meaning of the revolution in Catholic theology are fundamental. What he regards as a revolution—the restoration of theology on a sound methodological basis—I consider a reaction to the revolution in scientific method which has resulted in the emergence of the science of religious studies. Whereas he bases his conclusion upon the assumption that the Church can assimilate modern culture, I claim that the Church is an integral part of the classical and medieval tradition outmoded in the process of modernization. And while he compares the present revolution in theology to the medieval invention of theology, I think the modern revolution in Western culture is comparable to the beginning of the Christian era. Thus Father Lonergan expects the revolution to result in the restoration of theology within a renewed Christian culture, but I think a new era has begun to create its own appropriate mode of understanding the implications of ultimate meaning.

9   Commentary on "Revolution in Catholic Theology"

If I understand Fr. Lonergan's position correctly, it might be summarized in this way: The causes of vast changes in Catholic theology in the present century lie in the fact that the old (or classicist) style of dogmatic theology has now been eliminated, 1) by what amounts to a knowledge or information explosion that calls for great specialization; 2) by the acceptance of the obvious fact of cultural pluralism; 3) by acknowledgement of man's historicity; 4) by a new notion of science that is not rooted in metaphysics and the necessary. As a result, science in the future, and this includes theology, will be rooted in the cognitional and the psychological, with a stress on the importance of conversion and on the role of deliberating, evaluating, deciding and loving. The change that is going on is comparable to the transformation of theology in the twelfth and thirteenth centuries. I agree with almost all of what Fr. Lonergan has said—but for discussion purposes, I will concentrate on areas where I have some disagreements or on matters that he has not mentioned which seem to me to be significant for his topic, in the following seven comments:

1) I am not sure that what has been described here amounts to a *genuine revolution* in Catholic theology, although this may be a matter of semantics. Up till now, it has been easier to provide a critique of past methods and a list of things that have been abandoned than it is to describe what has emerged that is of real worth—this seems to be true of Fr. Lonergan's presentation which is much clearer on what is disappearing or apparently discredited than on what is to replace it as a viable form of theology.

2) His stress throughout is on change in methodology, and perhaps for this reason he has *not dealt with a revolution in content* of theology *and in approaches* to content. On this basis, he has not mentioned a number of factors which seem to me to be at least as significant for the far-reaching changes that have taken place in Catholic theology and its methodology as the ones he lists. I would like to add four more elements in this revolution: 1) an emphasis on humanism, with a stress on the *continuity* of the Christian message with secular values in this world—in contrast to a theology that would emphasize a dichotomy between spiritual and secular values, in contrast as well to a theology that would emphasize the need for redemption from sin, in contrast finally to a theology that would lay stress on the future life; this can lead and has lead to a tendency to reject any conclusion whose reasonableness cannot be *fully* verified both in itself and in its consequences; 2) a separation of prayer and personal holiness from the study of theology, with a consequent de-emphasis of the doctrine of grace; this can easily reduce theology to a set of abstract principles or a study of human history; 3) a stress on the importance of involvement with current issues, and on theology's immediate practical consequences or lack of them—which leads easily to an identification of truth and relevance, to the detriment of both; 4) a questioning of the theologian's relationship to the organized Church, or to official Church authorities—which at times leaves theologians with what Charles Davis described recently as free-floating personal ideologies—I don't think that the current situation in Catholic theology can be considered realistically without taking these elements into account.

3) His treatment of *pluralism and historicity* is accurate and useful but it does not point up the critical problem facing Catholic theologians, and the Church as a whole, in this area now: —Not whether to admit pluralism and historicity or reject it— but rather how to determine what must be permanent and lasting in the Christian message if it is to be truly Christian in an age of rapidly shifting cultures and situations.

4) I would simply ask Fr. Lonergan if he is fully convinced

that the undeniable *swing away from metaphysics* that he has described is a *lasting* phenomenon—since there are some evidences in our society already of a disenchantment with the results of empiricism.

5) Lonergan seems to me to *underestimate the importance of the Church, the faith community, in theological development.* The old-style theologian may have seemed to be using proofs that covered a vast area and to be presenting them as conclusive, as if he had full command of his subject, but the picture was not really what it seemed. First, what he proposed was the fruit of scholarly work of many people. (I never met the theologian a generation ago who had full personal control of even most of his material.) But, much more to the point, what he was really doing was basing his teaching and conclusions not so much on his scholarship and evidence (even when he said that was what he was doing and really believed it himself). What he was really doing was articulating the current living faith of the community (in part) and serving as a spokesman for it, becoming a polemicist for it (even when he was invoking arguments from the past rather than the present to establish a position), a systematizer of it—and finally, serving as a source of growth in it (along with many other sources in the life of the Church), but this last role was filled less frequently and less significantly than he imagined. In short, he was more dependent on the faith of the community than he realized, more dependent on it than it was on him and his colleagues. The critical problem for a Catholic theologian now is the same as it was twenty years ago, and it is not how to control all the material or to attain full knowledge. If so, he could make no significant statements about doctrine till the last historical or sociological or exegetical datum had been run through the biggest computer. Instead, it is how he can authentically articulate the faith of the Church as it is being lived and help it to grow. This is a more complicated work now than twenty years ago, but it is still one he carries out in profound dependence on the Church rather than the reverse. Theology survives and thrives because faith communities, i.e. churches, care enough about it to make it important.

6) I may be badly misreading him here, but Fr. Lonergan seems to me to delineate theological developments *too much in terms of the mental processes of theologians and not enough in terms of the whole life of the Church.* The definition of the dogma of the Assumption of the Blessed Virgin Mary in 1950 had two important consequences for the methodology of Catholic theology: 1) It forced us to break with the commonly held view that all development in our understanding of the faith comes through a logical process carried on by theologians—and it made us much more conscious of the operation of the Spirit in ways that are much more complex than syllogistic reasoning. 2) It made us aware of the fact that the experiential contribution of the faithful might be much more significant for development of doctrine in many areas than the formal studies of theologians. It seems to me that both of these notions are obscured in the approach adopted here, and I simply ask if an old and questionable framework for explaining the development of doctrine, with too much emphasis on the intellectual and logical, is being retained.

7) Finally, Fr. Lonergan is *more sanguine* on the course of the current Catholic revolution in theology than I am—It may be the forerunner of a golden age, as the new methods of the twelfth century led to the glories of the thirteenth, but at this point, I see some resemblance to the decay of the fourteenth with its stress on nominalism and subjectivism and its all-embracing criticism that paid little attention to the positive riches of the Christian message. I hope that Fr. Lonergan is right and I am wrong.

10   Making One's Own Act Another's

JOHN T. NOONAN, JR.

My subject is "Church Law and the Humanization of Man."
I shall address it in terms of a problem which is fundamental
to law—the circumstances in which one person's act counts as
another's. In this usage, the creation of law, lie opportunities for
perverse debasement and for the charitable expansion of goodness.
I propose to look at the ways in which the law of the Church
has affected realization of these opportunities by Christians in
four kinds of legal institutions—slavery, trusteeship, agency,
and marriage. These instances both reflect concepts of God and
become means for an understanding of God, so that the law
here is penetrated by theology and interpenetrates theology in turn.

First, as to slavery, whose legal structure as an institution
perhaps needs to be emphasized. Slavery is not a relation of brute
power like the act of capture or kidnapping in which it may
originate. As a going system it is dependent on law in a variety
of ways—to classify the slaves as distinct from free persons,
to assimilate their distribution to the distribution of property,
to provide general directions for their movements, to assign punish-
ments for their breaches of public order, to regulate their sexual
and educational opportunities, and to dispose of their offspring.
Slavery, the use of one person so that his act counts as his master's,
works only through the conceptual genius, the cataloguing power,
the metaphor-making capacity of law.

In the Mediterranean world in which Christianity appeared,
slavery was almost as pervasive an institution as marriage and
a more pervasive institution than lending at usury. Christian law
transformed marriage, it condemned usury, but it ameliorated
slavery without transforming it or condemning it. Justinian, the
greatest of Christian theocratic lawgivers, taught that it was

"better to emancipate men than to enslave them"; but his legislation, understood by him to be the faithful execution of the will of the Most Holy Trinity, confirmed the institution of slavery which pagan Rome had adopted and earlier Christian emperors had left undisturbed.

On two points imperial Christian decrees showed sensitivity to the personhood of slaves. Prohibitions were directed at the proselytizing of slaves and at their sexual exploitation; in both cases those protected were orthodox Christians. Heretical masters were forbidden to proselytize Christian slaves. Avaricious masters were forbidden to sell them to brothels. But Christians never enacted into Roman law the legal possibility for a slave to marry. Limited evidence does indicate that the Pope, against opposition by parts of the comunity, recognized that slaves could marry within the Church; and in the very long run—over 1000 years after the beginning—the sensitivity to the sexual rights of the slave culminated in Gratian's ringing declaration that, as there was neither slave nor free man in Christ Jesus, slaves could marry validly against the will of their masters.

It would be foolish to minimize the importance of Christian insistence on a zone of personal sexual integrity within the conditions set by slavery; it would be myopic to overlook the encouragement which Christian example and Christian Roman law gave to the emancipation of slaves "in the bosom of the Church." But the great fact cannot be disregarded that the institution of slavery was not challenged by those most qualified to attack its assumptions and its concepts, the Christian lawgivers and lawyers. Christian law did not create this dehumanizing institution, but it failed spectacularly to criticize it.

It is easy—possibly too easy—to explain the Roman Christians' attitude to slavery by the Platonic and Stoic elements in their thought, by their other-worldly outlook and belief that all would be compensated for in heaven. After all, usury was a social evil which was not accepted with resigned indifference but was vigorously combatted in patristic thought. Nor can the acceptance of slavery in the Old Testament alone account for the Christian conscience which so sharply rejected such Old Testament institutions as polygamy. Nor do St. Paul's words—"Slaves, obey your masters" (Eph 6:5)—and his exhortation to a fugitive slave to return (Philem 12) by themselves explain the lack of a Christian critique; Paul's words are more a part of the attitude to be explained than reason for it. Stoicism, Platonism, other-wordly orientation, Old Testament institutions, and Pauline texts do indeed cohere together, and in combination provide a partial theological explanation of the Christian position but two theologically-molded beliefs seem to me of special importance in the Christian acceptance of slavery as a legal institution. The first is that it was not inconsistent with being a person to be a slave— essential personhood was not lost or violated or damaged by the condition. This belief is most vividly illustrated in the analogical application of the term "slave" to monks. The slave was property-less, wifeless, will-less; so too was the monk, who was the slave of God. The application of the term "slave of the slaves of God" to the Pope, rhetorical as the usage soon became, reflected the same conviction. Behind both applications stood the precedent of Paul; Jesus himself, in the Pauline formula, in becoming man had "taken the form of a slave." The view of the human person here did not make it inappropriate to express the Incarnation itself in terms of becoming a slave. Slavery as a legal institution could not be attacked until a different vision of the human person had become dominant.

The other vital belief bore on the moral justification of slavery. Enslavement in battle was a moral corollary of accepting the possibility of just war. In the actual fighting it was a humane alternative to killing. But how could the enslavement of the children of captives be defended? Why was this weakest point in the institution of slavery not attacked? Why did Christian law accept without demur the axiom of classic law that status followed birth?

Here, it seems to me, theological influence was decisive. Men inherited Adam's state by birth. Original sin was fundamental to the Pauline explanation of man's fallen state. The doctrine of inherited status was essential to orthodox theology. With that view of the nature of creation, it was difficult to object to the civil law's analogous assumption that one's fate was determined by one's father. The metaphor of slavery was invoked by Paul himself in explaining man's redemption. The transmission of slavery by inheritance—vital to the working institution of slavery, morally its weakest point—did not seem open to challenge by Paul or by the Christian legislators when they came to imperial power.

The consequences of the lack of a Christian legal critique of slavery need little enlargement. Grant, if one will, that radical transformation of the social structure of the Roman Empire was impossible even under Christian rule. Grant, if one likes, that the lot of slaves held by monasteries and bishops well into the Middle Ages was not appreciably worse than the rural villeinage of free serfs. The Christian failure—the absence of a set of mind formed by law which made slavery as repugnant as polygamy, the absence of a legal doctrine that persons could not be property —came home to roost when the New World was discovered and enemy Indians in it were enslaved and when they did not suffice were supplanted by the Africans. Slavery in the Western world which lasted until little more than a century ago owed its beginnings to the men of Spain, Portugal, France, the Netherlands, and England, all nations molded by Christian thought. The occasional sharp protests of churchmen against unjust enslavement of Indians or against the brutalities of the African slave trade were no substitute for an entrenched legal critique of the very possibility of transmissible human slavery. The omissions of Church law left open gulfs of dehumanization into which European civilization plunged, in which American civilization foundered.

I turn now to consider an apparently happier relationship in which one man's act may become another's, that of the trustee or independent fiduciary. In the paradigmatic legal form the trustee acts only for the benefit of what the law calls his cestui que trust or beneficiary. What he makes of the trust property he does not make for himself, and his actions as trustee are never for his own account but for another's. In the same way a laywer must act for his client, in the performance of his function putting first not himself but him for whom he acts. Analogously, within limits less strictly defined by law, officials of a government are trustees for the people, supposed to act not for their own advantage but for that of their cestui que trust. As government is a natural necessity and as there will always be those who because of tender or advanced age or illness cannot act for themselves, so vicarial responsibility for others is required by the human condition. Parents are natural vicars. Civil law has supplemented them by guardians, church law by godparents. To find dangers in the concept of vicarage is not to suggest that it could be dispensed with, nor to overlook the exercise of altruism often present in providing for the wants of another by attributing to him an act of one's own.

Unlike the slave, the fiduciary is not smaller than the one for whom he acts, but larger. In the exercise of his trust it is his judgment that he is expected to follow. He is more qualified or more experienced or more talented than the beneficiary who reaps the fruit of his skill. There is no question of the beneficiary instructing him in the discharge of his function, no danger that he will be extinguished as a person by mechanical subordination to his cestui que trust. The relation, nonetheless, creates a risk to the trustee's integrity as a person. The risk arises because the one who acts vicariously for another may assume a moral position distinct from that of an individual person. If the risk is not avoided, the vicarious benefactor will dispense himself from many of the obligations of personal morality in the execution of his task. The altruism of his objective will become excuse for the amorality of his action.

Lawyers are a familiar illustration of this kind of conversion from personal to vicarial morality. It is not infrequently supposed in the profession that a lawyer owes his client every service compatible with justice, that he may virtuously do for his client acts which he would find selfish or heartless if he were to perform them on his own account. As an officer of the court he is expected to observe the requirements of justice, but in his professional role he may and perhaps must dispense with other virtues such as charity, patience, and humility. It is in that spirit in which eminent lawyers of the past such as Thomas Jefferson and Abraham Lincoln maintained by their professional work the American system of slavery while privately deploring its existence. It is in that spirit that eminent lawyers of today regard the substantive business of a corporation as no concern of theirs when they are engaged in furthering its growth by their discharge of a technical task. Their professional capacity is a carapace armoring them against judgments of morality. Acting for another, they confine their moral responsibility to fidelity in execution of their trust.

The same phenomenon has always been apparent in the behavior of government officials. Persons who in their private relations with others are distinguished by their empathy, their forbearance, and their kindness may behave with astounding savagery in their actions undertaken for the commonweal. Winston Churchill may stand as a well-known example. Fairness, forgiveness, and charity characterized him in treating persons he knew as private individuals. As a governmental official he was capable of cruelty to individuals and to groups, culminating in the monstrous action of directing the destruction of over a hundred thousand persons living in Dresden on St. Valentine's Eve, 1945.

The history of the Church could be written in terms of the blunders, crimes, and tragedies justified by the morality of vicarious responsibility. That familiar parade of terrible examples—the Inquisition, the Crusades, the Wars of Religion—could be analyzed in terms of it. It is difficult to identify in these vast institutional aberrations malevolent men; it is not difficult to find saints who thought that what they did for another had to meet a less rigorous standard than what they did for themselves. At the heart of Church law the justifying formula was put succinctly by the Father of the Canon Law in his discussion of the use of force. Referring to the vengeful acts of Pope Silverius, Gratian said, "But by these acts he avenged not his own injury but that of the Church." The vicar was credited with a morality different from the man; he was given the armor, the carapace to shield him from the moral pain of choosing as a man.

The Church officeholder was not only a fiduciary, he was God's representative; the Pope, God's vicar. It was no human cause he avenged, no human cause he fought for, no human justice he enforced. The theology instilling these concepts of the special relation of the officeholder to God swelled the status of the ecclesiastical fiduciary beyond mere human trusteeship. It magnified without essentially altering the split between the trustee as a man and the trustee as benefactor of another.

As the examples indicate, it has often been not the worst of men but the best who in fidelity to a vicarial office have put aside personal responsibility and moral sensitivity—the Jeffersons, Lincolns, and Churchills; and they have been able to find precedents and paradigms of their actions in the actions of officeholders of the Church. Their justification may be found in the classic texts of canon law. In this way, by example and by precept, by institutional law bolstered by theology, the Church fostered the view that he who acts for another may do for the other what he may not do for himself.

Vicarial responsibility of a different kind was at the same time exercised within the Church. In prayer Christians asked to be heard on behalf of others; saints became patrons and advocates. Sometimes ways of life followed ways of thought, and Christians became poor to aid the poor, sick to help the sick; the Mercederians even substituted themselves as slaves to redeem the slaves. The model of such action was the vicarious sacrifice of Jesus.

In this kind of substitution for another, more power was not claimed because of the vicarial role, but more was sacrificed of oneself. The moral demand was greater, not less. Vicarial action became, at its limit, the voluntary assumption of the shape of a slave. The vicar was preserved from dehumanizing himself by surrender of himself. The theological vision which made institutional slavery acceptable simultaneously purged vicarial action of selfishness. Can a Christian make his act another's without grave moral risk only by the sacrifice of himself as a person?

A third and general way of putting oneself in the place of another is agency. Slaves and fiduciaries too may be viewed as agents; I speak now of neither as such but of the free person who acts without great discretion at the direction of another, making his act count as the other's. How does free and limited agency of this kind relate to the personhood of man?

Suppose two lists of human acts of which one consists of

Buying, Selling, and Paying; Making Contracts; Marrying; Arguing in Court; Making War; and the other consists of Eating; Sleeping; Copulating; Knowing; Loving. What is the basis of distinction between them? The first list starts on a commercial note but is expanded to include transactions which may be completely un-commercial. The second list begins with the immediately physical but is extended to include complicated spiritual processes. The difference, I suggest, is that the first kind of acts are those where it is generally accepted that one person may be an agent for another, the second those which are commonly regarded as uniquely personal, so that no agent may carry them out for his principal. You may marry by proxy, but you may not have intercourse by proxy. You may hire a soldier to fight for you, but not a slugabed to sleep for you. You may have a lawyer represent you in court but not a professor represent you in an examination. In one set of instances the act done in your name is as good or better than if you had done the act yourself in person; in the other the inter-vention of an intermediary seems to be absurd.

The distinction between the delegable and the undelegable is also the distinction between the legal and the nonlegal. In each case where another may act for you a legal concept has made the literally impossible metaphorically appropriate so that you, not being present in body, may make your agent's act your own. The necessity of a legal concept is particularly plain where the deleg-ability of an act is uncertain or contested—cooking, for example, or teaching. If the hostess bakes the cake herself, it may well be looked at in a different light by herself and her guests than if she had bought it at the bakery, although in either case in serving it she may speak of it as part of "her dinner"; if the cake were the work of her cook, ascription of responsibility to her would be even more delicate and debatable. Teaching may be assigned by a professor to be conducted by section leaders in a course he is classified as teaching; it will often be felt that he has engaged in unwarranted fiction. No definite concept of agency has developed which definitively authorizes the hostess to treat her cook's act as her own or the professor his assistants'. Only where a legal concept has been accepted as appropriate is it possible for one person to stand in for another.

As definition suggests and as these examples manifest, the legal concept of agency will be acceptable only where what is done is thought not to require any special personal quality. The introduction of agency is depersonalizing. Sometimes, no doubt, this may be counted a gain, as when lawyers were substituted for litigants in lawsuits or when trial by battle became possible by hired champions. But it is a gain in such instances only because the personal relations were hostile. In the general run of cases where persons are aiding each other, the use of an intermediary means a loss in knowledge, in love, in reciprocal recognition of humanity.

Agency, nonetheless, is a necessity of large communities. It requires but a moment's thought to imagine what commercial chaos would occur if every owner had to sell in person, how corporations would disappear without agents to act for them, how government itself could not operate without delegated functionaries. A world without agents able to act for their principals would be so remote from our experience that it would be Utopian to speculate upon its structure. The legal concepts of delegation, proxy, agency have permitted men to organize their activities, extend their power, and build their communities in multiple ways beyond the boundaries which would hold if persons had to relate to each other in person.

The Gospel itself is rich in appeals to agency: "He who hears you, hears me." "Whatever you shall bind on earth shall be bound in heaven, and whatever you shall loose on earth shall be loosed in heaven" (Mt 18:8). The texts are not only the ecclesiological ones: "Whoever receives one such child for my sake, receives me" (Mt 18:5). "As long as you did it for one of these, the least of my brethren, you did it for me" (Mt 25:40). In all of these instances persons are put in the position of Christ, acting and receiving for him.

Canon law, while it did not create these concepts, has fostered them, and their expansion and their pervasiveness in Western thought is owed to the Church's sponsorship. Distribution of authority in the hierarchical organization was largely accomplished by agency. Consistent with a theology which emphasized the descent of power from God to the Church, from the Apostles to the bishops, from Peter to the Pope, delegation was a favored mode of action. Judges-delegate judged for the Pope throughout the world. Bishops dispensed by papal permission. Curates witnessed marriages by their pastor's delegation. Everywhere canon law favored the use of surrogates. It gave cathedral chapters, monasteries, universities and the Church itself the structure of a corporation.

None of this organization and extension of power was possible without a vision of human solidarity and communal responsibility. The channels which were made for cooperative human effort, the perduring shapes which were given to intellectual and religious endeavors, must be counted as the fruits of the depersonalizing of human acts by agency. Collectively formed by legal forms has been the condition for the conduct of research, the dissemination of knowledge, and the life of the religious order.

Sacramental theology, especially as developed in scholasticism, sought to explain divine cooperation with human action in the sacraments in terms of instrumental causality. Is not the law of agency the model on which this metaphysical notion is based? When he consecrates the bread and wine, the priest acts not in his own name but Christ's. The minister of any sacrament becomes so by subordinating his intention to the Church's. The participants in the liturgy do not intend to join the celebrant in his own person; the recipients of the sacraments want to encounter Christ, not the priest in his human qualities. If the legal concept did not exist that an agent's act may be attributed to his principal without personal liability by the agent, the Church would have had to invent it; for the ministers of the sacraments act for their divine principal without personal liability for their acts. Marriage, of course, is an exception. Putting it aside, the sacramental system has depended on the depersonalization of the distributors of sacramental grace, so that through the act of any priest God could act.

The sacrament which most strikingly combines agency and

personal participation is penance. On the one hand, the hearing of confession is reserved to those delegated jurisdiction by the bishop, and in pronouncing absolution these priests act not in their own name but God's. On the other hand, the personal participation of the penitent is required. The sacrament of penance has developed by analogy to a court; it is the internal forum, where the priest acts as judge; but representation by counsel is forbidden. Nothing in sacramental theory as such justifies this rule. Marriage, after all, may be sacramentally contracted by proxy. Vicarious reparation has been dominant in the theology of redemption. Commutation of corporeal penances to cash fines has been an established practice in the past. Why could one not confess his sins and sorrow by an attorney and do penance through a professional penitent? In the collective reception of absolution a move is made in this direction. Is it only habit that makes the introduction of attorneys for the penitent seem grotesque?

Marriage, like agency, has been so often taken for granted as part of the order of things, that it requires a wrench of thought to realize to what extent it is a creation of law. No doubt without law male and female would live together, but if law did not designate particular words and actions as betokening the public commitment of a man and a woman to each other, how would marriage be distinguished from other forms of sexual association? As much as slavery, trusteeship, or agency, marriage depends upon a legal system for its definition and for recognition of its constituent elements.

Two peculiarities of marriage in the sacramental system of agency have been remarked. God's agents can delegate their functions to proxies. At the same time it matters who the agents are. If there is a mistake as to the person marrying, the marriage is invalid and the sacrament not conferred. The ministers of the sacrament do not merely bestow it; they are implicated by their action; they are personally involved by their agency. The possibility of proxy marriage is no doubt a minor anomaly, a survival from a time when marriage was more of a family treaty and less of an individual commitment, and now destined to be eliminated entirely as a fuller conception of marriage becomes dominant. But the other special features of sacramental marriage—that it depends on who the ministers are and that it makes the ministers liable for their act—seem neither trivial nor anachronistic. They demonstrate that depersonalized agency is not essential to the sacramental system. God does not have to impart grace by interchangeable ciphers.

If humanization of man means an increase in those acts which only an individual man can do—not only eating, sleeping, and copulating, but loving and knowing, then the role of Church law in humanizing man must be to increase the personal and to reduce the impersonal. How often the exception to a rule carries the true principle. Might marriage become the model of the responsibility entailed by the conferring of a sacrament? The ministers of this sacrament freely undertake to create the image of another relationship. Their union is a sign—visible only if embodied in their actions as human persons. Are they at the extremity of madness or have they reached the height of human insight, if, in the freedom of their mission, they say with Lear:

> We two alone will sing like birds i' the' cage;
> When thou dost ask me blessing, I'll kneel down
> And ask of thee forgiveness; so we'll live
> And pray, and sing, and tell old tales, and laugh
> At gilded butterflies . . .
> And take upon's the mystery of things
> As if we were God's spies. . . .

Is agency the best concept to explicate such a relation or any sacramental relation of the members of the Christian community to one another and to Christ? Marriage, if it is taken as the model, provides a different paradigm: it functions not as slavery, trusteeship, or agency, but as a meeting of two who are representative by analogy, whose actions by mutual consent become one another's.

In Genesis we are told that man is made in a likeness. In the Gospels, likeness is carried to a sublime degree: "he who sees me sees also the Father" (Jn 14:9). The concept is not one of agency. It may be that sayings such as "Whoever receives one such little child for my sake, receives me" should be understood analogously, not in terms of agency, but of likeness. Even the ecclesiological texts—"He who hears you"; "Whatever you shall bind"—may be patient of this reading. Focus then is directed to the person acting as conformed to the person of Christ. The classic phrase, *alter Christus,* captures the sense.

Slavery, trusteeship, and agency are legal constructions which make human interaction possible by substitutes treating one person as larger or smaller than another. One side of Christian thought, accepting the inequalities and distances inherent in the relations of people, has made the best of them by such palliatives. For this thought the human encounter is possible only by such fictions, such games; the real events are extraterrestrial. The other side of Christian thought has stressed the unique character of each life on earth, and perceived each unique being here as linked to others by the bonds of love. For it, too, however, man does not stand by himself, but as an image. In the language of St. John, we are no longer addressed as slaves, but as friends. Our acts are another's not by legal fiction but by likeness.

11 Commentary on "Making One's Own Act Another's"

FREDERICK R. MCMANUS

With his usual thoughtfulness and insight, Professor Noonan has placed before us instances of church law which may be humanizing or dehumanizing. I will content myself with offering some brief observations on church law as an instrument of reform within the Church community—we may hope that such reform is in the direction of humanizing.

First, the church law may be a means to strengthen and structure the community of believers. Public attention has been caught by the current effort at a fresh redaction of that part of the canon law which appeared as a code for the Western Church in 1917. But that effort at codification is entirely secondary, it is mere busy work, compared to the actual change of the institutes of church order—by the enactments of the Second Vatican Council, by subsequent decrees of the pope and conferences of bishops, and legislated norms within the local churches. The bylaws of a pastoral or presbyteral council; the creation of new officers of responsibility and service within the diocesan community; the canonical emergence of a kind of new Roman Curia (the secretariats, the Commission for Justice and Peace, the Council of the Laity); the gradual—many would say too gradual—reworking of norms affecting mixed marriage and eucharistic sharing; the carefully thought out institution of the permanent diaconate; the reform of sacramental celebration in the Latin Church, in the national churches, in the local churches, to the extent that such celebration can be fixed by norm or rule—these are instances where the church law is a tool in current reform.

Some of these canonical developments merely reflect the necessities of the moment or result from strong pressures within the

Christian community. Sometimes they are created in the first place by the making of statutes and decrees. Sometimes they are deductions from principles, for example, the principles of human dignity and freedom or of general participation in political, social, and cultural life. Such principles were enunciated in conciliar documents, although most of the conciliar fathers hardly expected them to be directly applicable within the church community.

A recent paper on Innocent III's definition of marriage raised the question whether the pope intended to influence social change in the direction of personal, individual responsibility and even in the direction of clandestine marriages. Was his doctrine of marital consent planned to weaken the role of parents, families, overlords, and perhaps the ministers of the Church in favor of the individual persons? The question itself may not be susceptible of historical proof one way or the other, but it may illustrate a point about canonical reform.

Change in church order and discipline may come about because of circumstances inside and outside the church society. In the example of Innocent III there were surely influences and forces in medieval society, law, and church life to explain the pope's position. But there is also the possibility of conscious, deliberate initiative on his part to employ the canon law for change or to use it as a means to channel, guide, or deflect change already at work.

This conscious initiative may be the role of a church legislator (pope or bishop) or of a church legislature (council or conference or synod). What is new today is that those who practice church law, at least in the English-speaking world, are seeking and occasionally finding a real place in the legislative process. Practicing canonists are consciously involving themselves in the use of church law as a means to humanizing reform.

At times the process does not work well or work at all. For example, a fundamental difficulty in the aborted *schema* of Fundamental Law was that church office holders would have employed the law to lessen their accountability to those whose servants or slaves they are. Sometimes canonical legislation is as little responsive to the needs of the community or the hopes of its members as is the United States Congress on the matter of gun controls. This is where the analogy of civil and canon law is at its most painful, and it suggests another point I would like to make.

Second, Professor Noonan has referred to a particular problem of the concept of vicarious responsibility within the Church. This problem could also be characterized as a hierarchical self-identification with the Church. The danger is that those who are scrupulous to avoid transgressions in their personal lives can act arbitrarily, inequitably, and uncanonically in their leadership positions within the Church. A partial remedy is now projected, namely, administrative tribunals to hear recourse against administrative decisions of the Church's ministers. But there are altogether too many lost opportunities of reform, if only the Church's ministers had fully respected the law they expect the rest of the Christian community to observe.

This failure to respect the church law ranges all the way from neglect of canonical principles of non-retroactivity, promulgation, and interpretation to simple violations of law, for example, lack of consultation in appointment of parochial vicars, refusal of ministry by judges, neglect of synods and councils, and neglect of the very principle of synodical governance, uncanonical centralization of property administration, imposition of penalties without process. It is curious, for example, to see contemporary testing and evaluation procedures for orders and church offices when the old-fashioned canons which have the same purpose have been neglected or treated as mere formalities by the Church's ministers.

A more serious example is the recent pastoral norms for penance. These seem never to have heard of the conciliar rule for communal celebration of sacraments. This rule is surely somehow applicable to the rite of reconciliation and peace with the Church.

The conciliar law of Vatican II, again, determined once for all the clear location of pastoral responsibility for church order and discipline as within the local church. Since the council, with the exception of the minor matter of the dispensing power of bishops, this norm has been hardly noticed in the making of church law.

My second point, then, is a comonplace. Whatever the excesses of legalism, however great the need to improve the articulation of church order, discipline, and rights in fewer rules and canons, it is not always the law that is at fault. Too often it is the ordained ministers and servants who do not respect the rule of law. For the rest of the Christian people this makes of law a dehumanizing burden.

In recent years the canon law has been in some disrepute, partly because of excesses or obsolescence in the law, partly (I fear) because of an irrational longing for simplicity that may only mean disunity or chaos. I think Professor Noonan, as a lawyer, will agree that the church law can be a means to reform, a check upon the Church's ministers, and an instrument of unity and human, Christian solidarity.

12   Monasteries, Universities, and Seminaries and the Development of Roman Catholic Moral Theology

ROBERT G. KLEINHANS

Many Protestants, and a growing number of contemporary Roman Catholics, complain that they do not understand traditional Roman Catholic moral theology. Its controlling themes, its mode of operation, and its underlying presuppositions elude their comprehension. These persons may resemble those Englishmen whom Chesterton tells us complain that they do not understand American politics, when they would be more truthful if they admitted that they did not understand English politics. But there is still some justification for this inability to comprehend Roman Catholic moral theology. One way in which to come to a better understanding of this "mystifying" discipline is to review its history in terms of its mental and socio-cultural environment: i.e., the structures of consciousness of which it is a part and the socio-cultural institutions which served as the loci of its development: medieval monasteries, the medieval cathedral schools, the medieval universities, and Post-Tridentine seminaries. That is the purpose, if not the accomplishment, of the following presentation.

ELEMENTS OF A CHRISTIAN ETHIC

We must preface this discussion with a few brief reflections on Christian ethical thought itself. The major elements of reflection upon Christian living may be loosely classified under three major headings.

First there is the reflection upon the resources available to the individual Christian for ethical action, the dynamic energy necessary for the actual ethical action. While reflection upon this element of ethics has generally been relegated to the discipline commonly called dogatics or dogmatic theology, the distinction between dogmatic and moral theology is not complete and decisions taken in either discipline will have important effects upon elements in the other. In addition, while the reflections upon the energies available to the Christian for ethical action have generally been classified under the topics of original sin, the state of fallen men, justification, sanctification, and grace, we must remember that these parts of dogmatic theology are conditioned by and also condition orientations and doctrines associated with other parts of dogmatic theology such as creation, the Incarnation, the nature of God, and eschatology. The inter-relation of these considerations and the ultimate framework of thought supporting such considerations can be described as the structure of consciousness. Another aspect of the structure of cosnciousness is the structure of conscience from which ethical action proceeds. The structure of consciousness which organizes and colors our perception of the world, the human condition, and Christian destiny, obviously influences the structure of conscience.

This later element, the structure of conscience, may be divided into two major categories. First there is the reflection on the norms, principles, laws, or to use the more currently fashionable terms (and theologians should be fashionable, I suppose) reflection on the controlling themes, paradigms for action, directions or ethical orientations which determine ultimate moral values. This is not to assert that morals must have basic principles, divine laws, or eternal values as their basis but rather to indicate that reflection on human action seems to include the identification of norms, rules, or an orientation which should or will underlie ethical action. Even proponents of Christian situation ethics maintain that love, whatever that may be, should be a controlling theme, orientation, or driving force for all Christian action. This reflection on norms and principles for ethical action has generally been designated as moral theology and the history of that discipline is to a great extent the history of the various bases or norms which have been chosen to organize ethical thought: divine and natural law, moral and theological virtues, or the structures of grace itself.

The second element of the structure of conscience and the third element which we wish to discuss may be designated by a term now in much disrepute, if not total oblivion, *casuistry*: the science and art of applying the general norms of moral theology to concrete situations. Also associated with this element of moral reflection are the aids to the care of souls: the guides to Christian living, the devotional literature which nurtures and sustains private prayer life, the liturgical and sacramental piety which frequently creates an ethos from which ethical action is to spring, and even the lost art of hagiography, an art which if it is to be recovered will, it is hoped, develop its prose style beyond that hybrid of ancient panegyric and contemporary bubble gum baseball cards with which it was too frequently associated in the more recent past.

But back to our categories. Since the twelfth century the structure of consciousness (by which and through which men perceive themselves, their world, their destiny, the resources available to them for fulfillment, salvation, and beatification) the structure of conscience (the norms or principles to which men appeal to organize, regulate, and evaluate ethical action), and casuistry (the procedures used to apply these norms to concrete situations) have been developing and changing within the Roman Catholic tradition. A knowledge of the history of this development assists in comprehending traditional Roman Catholic moral theology.

We have chosen to commence this study with the twelfth century not only because the cultural renaissance of this period did much to condition subsequent Western thought, or, as Chenu has so ably shown us, because theology during this period did become a science (or as we would say, a discipline) or, because as Benjamin Nelson assures us

> ... it is the Twelfth and Thirteenth Centuries—the era of the Crusades, of Western recovery of the Mediterranean, of expanded urban liberties and mass social heresies, of vernacular literature and the new Universities which witnesses the extraordinary advance of the new logic of conscience

and the emergence of a new system of administration of the care of souls. (Benjamin Nelson, "Self-Images and Systems of Spiritual Direction in the History of European Civilization" in **The Quest for Self-Control.** Ed. Samuel Z. Klausner. New York: The Free Press, 1965, p. 64 [48-103])

not only because of all the above reasons but also because to have chosen an earlier stage for the genesis of this presentation would certainly have prolonged its conclusion to coincide with or post-date the arrival of the eschaton, no matter how long that day might be delayed. Since most college professors are primarily engaged in teaching college students for whom the Korean War is more readily related to those of ancient Greece than that of Vietnam, I am sure that the twelfth century will be a sufficiently early date to ensure some semblance of historical development in the following presentation.

12TH CENTURY—BERNARD AND ABELARD

Two major figures of the early twelfth century were of course Bernard, Abbot of Clairvaux, and Abelard, Master of Theology at Paris. The debates between these two men are almost as fascinating and exciting as the pedagogy employed by the latter with his famous student Heloise. But, while the Victorian ethics of recent generations seem to have convinced the theologians of the heretical tendenciess of Abelard's thought less by his intricate syllogisms and bold presuppositions than by his indiscretion and Heloise's resultant delicate condition, Bernard's own debate with Abelard was clearly one about theology itself. Bernard sensed, identified, and opposed the new method of theology which Abelard exemplified. In this sense at least, (and I would say, alone) Bernard was the last of the Fathers and Abelard the foremost among the scholastics.

Following Anselm's model Abelard attempted to find the necessary reasons or inherent necessity of matters held by faith. Just as Anselm had attempted to find out not only why God had become man but why it was necessary for God to become man, Abelard attempted to show why there *had to be* a Trinity. Bernard objected to this method. The Abbot of Clairvaux viewed the Christian life as a response to the Spirit by whose illumination one penetrated beyond the symbols of the liturgy and the literal sense of the Holy Scriptures to find Christ who by his love for man drew the soul to follow him and to be transformed by the Spirit until, in loving embrace with Christ, he gazed with him in the Spirit upon the face of the Father. This was a far different world than that of Abelard where one reflected upon the necessary reasons and causes for the reality of the Trinity. In Abelard's world reason itself mastered the facts of faith, penetrated beyond the Trinity itself, rather than being drawn beyond itself in ecstasy and rapture to be transformed by the vision of the Father in the Son and through the Holy Spirit. And so for Abelard the ultimate guide in ethics was reason which determined the intention of the ethical act which in turn determined all ethical value. For Bernard, Christ was the ultimate norm and example of all Christian life; Christians were to follow the example of Christ in his Incarnation, his Death, and his Resurrection; Christians were to participate in the life of Christ. For Abelard, Christ was a teacher; His Birth, Death and Resurrection were added aids in teaching man the meaning of life; Christians were to reflect upon the mysteries of faith till they penetrated beyond them to the inherent causes of their necessity while man's reason itself ultimately determined ethical value.

For Bernard the ideal for a Christian was to live under a spiritual father, an abbot (preferably Bernard) and by penance (the kiss of the feet of Christ) and a life of virtue (the kiss bestowed upon Christ's hands) come to the mystical union (the kiss of the mouth) in which the soul was transformed into Christ. For Abelard the ideal for a Christian was to live under a philosopher, a Master of Theology (preferably Abelard) and by reflection and individual decision live the good life which prepared one for its eternal continuation after death. In both views the doctrine of morality was integrally related to dogma and the care of souls though the contrasts between the two structures of consciousness are obvious at every point. For Bernard it was a faith-structure of consciousness and conscience; for Abelard, a rationalized structure of consciousness and conscience; for Abelard, a rationalized structure of consciousness and conscience. (See Benjamin Nelson, "Civilizational Complexes and Intercivilizational Encounters," Paper delivered at the American Sociological Association Conference, Denver, Colorado, August 30, 1971.)

But for both Abelard and Bernard, the structure of consciousness was unified: dogma, moral principles, and the application of these principles to daily life were integrally united. This unity of mental structure was mirrored in the socio-cultural milieu of medieval monasticism and the cathedral schools. Monasteries were in fact local Christian communities and the monastic vocation, as Louis Bouyer and Dom. C. Marmion have so frequently reminded us, was nothing more than the vocation of the Christian. The cathedral schools were at most extensions of the local church. Both institutions, the monastery and the cathedral schools, were worms of the local church and theology was united by the unity which existed in the local church itself. While this is more true in the case of monasteries with their abbots who were the intellectual leaders and spiritual fathers of their monks, it was also true of the masters of the cathedral schools who originally were the local bishops. By the twelfth century these institutions were already losing their traditional structure and role. Bishops had long before ceased to serve as principal teachers in their schools. This job had been handed over to the masters while bishops dedicated their time to more lucrative or licentious pursuits. Nevertheless, the socio-cultural unity of the monasteries and the cathedral schools, rooted in the socio-cultural unity of the local church, paralleled the unity of the structures of consciousness already identified. And as Bernard's faith-structure of consciousness and conscience assisted in the latter stages of the transformation of the cathedral school into the medieval university, a transformation of that institution from an extension of the local church into an independent institution established by the free association or union of teachers, of teachers and students, or, as in the case of the earliest stages in Bologna, of students only. The universities actually became guilds providing for the personal pursuit of the study of theology, law, and medicine.

13TH CENTURY—MEDIEVAL UNIVERSITY

In this emerging institution, the medieval university, neither Bernard nor Abelard were to dominate. It was their contempoary, Peter the Lombard, who ultimately dominated the medieval university with his *Book of the Sentences,* or *Book of Opinions* as we should really call it, the theological best seller of the thirteenth century universities. The *Book of the Sentences* was completed less than a decade after Bernard triumphed over Abelard at the Council of Sens, and before the thirteenth century reached its first quarter mark Alexander of Hales had introduced this work at the University of Paris. The Bible and the Sentences became the works which each budding medieval theologian had to literally master. It was the structure of the *Sentences* that conditioned theology for at least three centuries.

Peter the Lombard set out to discuss theology under two general topics, the matters of faith and their signs. The first book discussed the Trinity; the second, creation, original sin, grace, virtue, and sin; the third, Christ; and the fourth, the sacraments, God's remedy for sin. The discussion of specific moral principles and Christian life, however, is not found in Book II on creation, man, and original sin, but as a sort of appendix to Book II on Christology. After discussing Christ's divine and human nature, the Lombard asks if Christ possessed the virtues of faith,, hope and charity. This leads to the discussion of these virtues, the gifts of the Holy Spirit, the two-fold commandment of love, and then the decalogue. In some respects Peter the Lombard seems to follow Bernard. Virtues are discussed under Christology, but Christ is not presented as the model for Christian virtue. Rather the discussion of Christ is the occasion for discussing virtues; it is discussed here to explain Christ's humanity, not to have Christ show man what he should be. There are echoes of Abelard here but the Lombard's presentation lacks the integration which theology seemed to have in Abelard's developed thought. Peter does imitate Abelard: The *Book of the Sentences* or *Book of Opinions* follows the tradition of Abelard's *Sic et Non;* Peter approaches the discussion of the Trinity not in view of scriptural revelation or mystical union by participation in the life of the Trinity, but by the analogy of the threefold nature of the soul; and he maintains that by intellectual intuition man can and has examined the invisible God through those things which have been made, his creatures. Despite these resemblances to Abelard, however, the Lombard never achieves Abelard's synthesis or unity of vision and the discussion of morality is not integrated into the theological framework, there is only a juxtaposition. The later clear distinction between moral and dogmatic theology is already discernible.

At the same time as this disjunction between dogma and morals was developing, theology was becoming a science, a discipline, a professional art if you will, which was divorced from the care of souls. The university, now the home of theology, was not a local church as the monastery was nor an extension of a local church as was the early cathedral school. Rather it was an institution which had its own chapel which further divorced it from the local church. In this setting theology was viewed as a science of what was believed and the symbols of these beliefs, and not necessarily the science of Christian living. This is one of the reasons why the very year, 1222, that the *Sentences* were adopted as a text at the University of Paris, Raymond of Pentafort, a canonist and not a theologian, began composing his *Summa de Poenitentia,* a very practical guide for caring for souls through the Sacrament of Penance. Unlike the early penitential books which merely matched particular penances to particular sins (a sort of lazy ecclesiastic's guide to moral bookkeeping), Raymond's work attempted to provide the priest confessor with doctrinal and canonical material in a practical digest useful for direction of souls through the confessional. There was certainly a need for such works since the Fourth Lateran Council ·established annual communion as a requirement for maintaining Church membership and priests had to be prepared to aid Christians through the annual confession which preceded the annual communion.

Thus by the thirteenth century casuistry and the care of souls, important elements of theology, no longer fell within the pale of theology or of its new locus in the university. Those works which dealt with the application of moral principles to life situations, the *Summa confessorum* developed outside of the university by canon lawyers rather than theologians and they are not found on the book list of the University stationer (the equivalent of the modern university book store's list of required texts). In addition, in the *Sentences* the strucure of conscience was not an integral part of the structure of consciousness. Aquinas realized this when he attempted to write a second Commentary on the *Sentences* and abandoned that project for the development of his own *Summa Theologica*. For Aquinas theology was a unity and morals actually dominated the theological task. Part II of the *Summa* became so extended that it had to be divided into IaIIae and IIaIIae. Certainly Aquinas maintained that the proper object of theology was God and all things in so far as God is their efficient and final cause, but he focuses his concern on man and his way of attaining his final end. Morals is the study of the image of God in man, namely freedom by which man is to return to God. There is more of Abelard here than Bernard and while Aquinas constantly attempts to subordinate reason to faith and nature to grace, he maintains that the ultimate matter of theology is not only what has been revealed but what is capable of revelation. For similar reasons the ultimate foundation of Christian morals is not God's revealed Will or Word, not law or virtues, but the structure of grace itself which fortifies the natural virtues and provides them with their necessary complements, the theological virtues without which man cannot be saved. The extent to which Aquinas developed this insight may be seen by his assertion that in one sense it was unfitting for the Law of the New Testament to have been written since in essence it consists in the grace of the Holy Spirit and not the codification of grace's urgings.

THE FRANCISCAN SCHOOL OF THE 14TH & 15TH CENTURIES

This attempt by Aquinas at unifying theology did not have much influence in the Middle Ages (or, one might add, at any other time, though several generations of theologians have claimed to be following in Aquinas' footsteps—rather large ones to fill no matter how we take the metaphor). Theology continued to grow within the framework of the medieval university and the *Sentences* of Peter the Lombard. Casuistry and the care of souls was excluded from theological discussions *per se* and dogmatic and moral theology exhibited increasing signs of developing as distinct disciplines. In the thirteenth century Alan of Lille was already suggesting that Theology was divided into two parts, that of the celestial (dogma) and that of the terrestrial (morals). In addition, the treatise on law and the decalogue began to become the center of ethical thought. Virtues were to be interpreted in terms of law; ethical values were established by the arbitrary will of God; the only foundation for morals was the decree of a properly constituted authority, God, King, or Bishop (though one suspects that the order was usually reversed and God came more and more to resemble the transcendent personification of the awesome, autocratic, ecclesiastic). We need only add that once law became the sole determinant of ethical values, obedience became the primary virtue and ultimate expression of love. This approach was particularly developed by the Franciscan school: Bonaventure's university works (though his other writings seem to follow the Bernardine tradition), Scotus, Ockham and ultimately Gabriel Biel. It was this school which could ultimately bring itself to say that if God commanded man to hate Him (God) it would be right for man to do so. This would have been blasphemy for Abelard, Bernard, or Aquinas. For Abelard God would have had to sponsor the natural virtues, one of which reason told us was piety and love of God; for Aquinas God's grace given to man in Christ could not contradict the very essence of God's own inner life which demanded that He love Himself and that all intellectual creatures love Him also; for Bernard man had to follow the example of Christ who loved the Father and drew man to Him by His own expressions of love revealed in Christ by the Holy Spirit.

Since the Nominalism of the fourteenth and fifteenth centuries rejected any *logos* or principle of order in things, it was logically forced to a revelation-faith basis for dogmatic theology and an authority-obedience basis for moral theology. Certainly these university theologians, unlike many subsequent father-confessors, insisted that the Law of Love held a priority over all other commandnments, but ethics or morals was now a question of law and obedience at all levels. It must also be noted that the division between theology and canon law which had developed at the end of the twelfth century had continued and by the mid-point of the fourteenth century the classical period of the development of canon law was ending. This discipline now was re-enforced by a philosophical and theological world view which placed authority, law, and obedience at the core of ethical life. The *Summa confessorum,* one of the fruits of the classical period of canon law, was now becoming the standard guide for confessors and some of these works were alphabetically arranged so that the priest could quickly and easily find the appropriate sin, penance, and cure with one easy reference. The professional clout of the new professionals in canon law also ensured the development of the trade and soon every religious house was to have a lecturer in canon law who would present monthly instruction in the discipline.

As we have seen, the distinction between dogmatic theology and moral theology at first clearly apparent in Peter the Lombard, became more clearly defined in the numerous commentaries on the *Sentences* which exemplified this tradition. The basic unity which remained was authority: authority of revealed doctrine in dogma and authority of revealed Law in morals. There was no possibility of ultimately perceiving the unity between doctrine and Law since law was essentially the result of the totally free will of the omnipotent Creator. God ruled His world with love, as revelation said, but there was no reason why he could not have done it differently or why he could not change His mind and do it differently. In short, God ruled His world as most college professors grade essay examinations, arbitrarily.

The break among the three elements involved in Christian ethics was almost complete. Casuistry was no longer a part of theology but assumed under canon law; morals and dogma were united only by the concept of authority; and ethical values were determined not by virtue in accordance with man's nature, nor by the structure of grace which was the nature of a Christian, nor by Christ's example, but by authority, primarily God's but also the Church's, though in actual practice we might expect that God's will seemed more benevolent and less arbitrary than that of the local ecclesiastic.

THEOLOGICAL MOVEMENTS BEYOND THE UNIVERSITIES

Outside of the structures of the medieval universities and the *Sentences* of Peter Lombard, however, there were several movements which were attempting to reunite dogma, morals, and the care of souls. They were also attempting to return to a faith-structure of consciousness and to replace the emphasis on law with the example of Christ. The *devotio moderna* in the Netherlands, the Rhineland, and at Montserrat in Spain, the Oratory of Divine Love in Italy, the Christian Humanism of the Northern Renaissance, each attempted to fuse these elements relating to Christian moral life into a unified whole; each resorted to a form of Neo-Platonism derived from the Rhineland mystics or the Florentine Academy; and each was associated primarily but not exclusively with social-cultural institutions beyond the pale of the university. While we have not time now to discuss these movements in great detail it seems to me that these movements rather than late medieval scholasticism are the key to the understanding of the various religious reforms of the sixteenth century, both Protestant and Roman Catholic, despite recent rumors to the contrary. It was these movements also which stimulated the educational reforms in Geneva, Wittenberg, and Rome: educational reforms which would cause the demise of the medieval university and the abandonment of the *Sentences* as the basic text of Theology.

MORAL THEOLOGY OF ROMAN CATHOLIC SEMINARIES

Within the Roman Catholicism of the 16th century the reform

of theological education was most closely associated with the Tridentine decrees on education of the clergy and the new religious orders which became associated with seminary education, particularly the Jesuits and the Sulpicians. The decree of the Council of Trent on the establishment of seminaries attempted to re-establish the cathedral school as a center for training priests. Once again theological studies were to be centered in an institution which was primarily an extension of the local church. Nevertheless the Tridentine seminaries developed quite differently from cathedral schools: first, only clerics studying for the priesthood were admitted as students, and secondly, the seminaries more frequently than not came under the control of religious orders and Roman Curial offices which supervised them. The organization and spiritual ethos of seminaries frequently owed more to the religious order and the Roman Curia than to the local church. In addition, according to Trent the seminary curriculum was to be composed of the liberal arts, the study of scripture and ecclesiastical authors, instruction in the rites, ceremonies, and censures of the Church, and preparation for the administration of sacraments, especially preparation for hearing confession, but it was never implemented in that form. Trent's decree was based on the proposals of Cardinal Pole who in turn was inspired by the Jesuit house of study in Rome. It was the Jesuit course of study and organization of seminary life which ultimately had more influence on seminary education and theological development than the actual program of Trent.

The 1599 Jesuit *ratio studiorum* indicated that each seminary was to have a Professor of the Cases of Conscience and a Professor of Scholastic Theology. The latter was to use Aquinas' *Summa Theologiae* rather than Peter the Lombard's *Sentences* as the basic theological textbook. Whenever possible all of the IaIIae which dealt with the principles of morals was to be considered; however, if there was only one professor of Scholastic Theology, he was to focus on those sections on morals which dealt with the end of man, sin, and law. The study of the virtues essential to Aquinas' understanding of how grace operated could be overlooked. In the IaIIae which dealt with the specific virtues, particularly the theological virtue bestowed by grace; the instructor was to focus on questions of justice, rights, and religion; only if time and personnel permitted would faith, hope and charity be discussed and then they were to share time with restitution, usury and contracts. This obviously indicates that one can easily adopt the *Summa* as a text without ever becoming a Thomist.

The Professor of the Cases of Conscience, on the other hand, would discuss the application of the above principles to particular cases, the sacramental rites, ceremonies, and censures of the Church, the duties pertaining to particular ecclesiastical states, and the commandments. This division of duties was soon altered, however, and the Professor of the Cases of Conscience took over the responsibility of summarizing the principles of morals leaving the Professor of Scholastic Theology to comment on the Ia and IIIa of *Summa,* the sections treating of God, creation, Christ, and the sacraments to which was soon added the section on grace, justification, and sanctification found in Ia IIae. The division between dogmatic theology and moral theology was complete. The new Moral Theology now consisted of an introductory section on the end of man, sin, and law to which were added the study of the cases of conscience, the rites, ceremonies, and censures of the Church, the duties of one's state, and the commandments of God and of the Church. This outline established a new genre of literature on morals, the *Institutiones Morales,* which from the mid-point of the seventeenth century set the basic framework for the discussion of moral questions within Roman Catholicism. Not only was the discussion of morals divorced from that of dogma but morality was now discussed primarily if not solely in terms of law and sin. The Jesuit H. Busenbaum penned what became the basic textbook of Moral Theology, his *Medulla Theologiae Moralis,* and Alphonsus Liguori's famous work on Moral Theology was meant, as the title pages of the early editions indicated as a commentary on Busenbaum. When the Jesuit order was suppressed, Liguori indicated that he had truly learned his Moral Theology from the

Jesuit school: he quickly supressed the citation of indebtedness to the Jesuit Busenbaum.

Let us return for a moment to the early seminaries. When the duties of the former Doctor of Theology of the medieval university were divided into two chairs of Professorships for the Seminary (the Professor of Sacred Scripture, and the Professor of Scholastic Theology), another part of his duties that related to Moral Theology was entrusted to the Professor of the Cases of Conscience. The man who assumed this Professorship was not a theologian but the former lecturer on canon law for religious houses who was mentioned earlier. The canon lawyer who previously trained persons to hear confessions by instructing them in ecclesiastical law now became the Professor of Moral Theology. This was the first entry of the canon lawyer into the faculty of Theology from whence he has yet to be removed.

The major debate on morality within Roman Catholicism during the seventeenth century was primarily a result of this new role of the Professor of the Cases of Conscience. The debate over probabilism was first of all a debate about the confessor's obligation when the penitent was unaware of the law. It later was extended to the forum of conscience itself. At that point, probabilism, the position associated with the Jesuits, maintained that if the law was unclear, one could follow any probable position, a stance which was to be identified with laxity by the Jansenists. Probabiliorism, espoused primarily by the Dominicans, maintained that in cases of doubt about the application of the law, one must follow the most probable position. The focus of this debate indicates not only that law was central to moral theology but that individual conscience was the ultimate determinat of ethical value for the individual conscience whenever there was a case of doubt—and the Probabilists should not be judged solely from the prejudiced perspective of Pascal and other partisans of Port Royal, they are responsible for the term Jesuitacal becoming a contemporary term for cunning, slippery dealing, and unprincipled ethical action.

While the probabilist controversy was partially the result

of the reintroduction of the consideration of the application of moral principles to individual situations to academic theological studies, it actually resulted in the practical exclusion of much of the discussion of the Christian life from moral theology and the seminary curriculum. This debate is primarily responsible for moral theology becoming the discussion of the minimal oblivation under law rather than one of the fullness of the Christian life. Once again this aspect of morals was disassociated from formal theological studies and the vast corpus of literature on the spiritual life so frequently associated with the seventeenth centrury developed primarily outside of the seminary curriculum which failed to incorporate it into its *ratio studiorum*. Only during the eighteenth century did the discipline of ascetical and mystical theology develop and it never acquired comparable status with dogmatic and moral theology within the seminary curriculum.

The seventeeth century formulation of Roman Catholic Moral Theology remained relatively permanent till the beginning of the twentieth century, despite some relatively slight influence of the Tübingen School of the nineteenth. This synthesis was characterized by:

First, the continued though less pronounced exclusion of the discussion of practical Christian life, Christian spirituality and the care of souls, from the academic study of theology;

Secondly, the further division of moral theology from dogmatic theology which became personified in the two chairs of dogmatic and moral theology in the Seminary; and

Thirdly, the affirmation of law and obligation as the basis of Christian morality.

The changes brought about by the twentieth century Thomistic revival and subsequent movements within Roman Catholicism lie beyond the limits of this presentation though it is hoped that this brief introduction to the history of Roman Catholic Moral Theology may help make its fascinating story more intelligible.

We shall terminate our survey of the History of Roman Catholic Moral Theology with this form of Moral Theology characteristic of post-Tridentine seminaries. Certainly from this time onward, the synthesis of dogma, morals, and the care of souls and Christian spirituality, so clear in the faith structure of consciousness of Bernard of Clairvaux and the rationalized consciousness of Abelard was nowhere evident. But the very development of the various theological disciplines as distinct and separate areas of learning has been viewed as a direct result of the rationalized-consciousness which lost the integration available in the faith vision of God. In the rationalized-conscience it is the forum of conscience rather than the example of Christ which ultimately determines ethical values and in the rationalized-consciousness it is the structures of the mental processes, the *ratio* of the intellect, rather than the *logos* within or beyond sensible reality which ultimately determines the structure of knowledge. In such a perspective there is little room for an approach to Christian life which maintains that the *logos* of reality is Christ Himself and that the *telos* or ultimate goal and meaning of existence lies beyond the very structure of the cosmos. While Bernard of Clairvaux's approach to Christian life is not the only, nor might I add from my perspective the best, form of asserting these values, it seems that this approach to Christian ethical reflection became increasingly less attractive to and less viable within Roman Catholicism.

13   Newman and Harnack: Conflicting Developments of Doctrine

WILLIAM J. HYNES

In the latter part of the nineteenth century, two of the most significant and influential attempts to account for seeming changes within the beliefs of Christianity were advanced by John Henry Newman and Adolf von Harnack. Although this issue occupied both men throughout their scholarly careers, each one's contribution has tended to become associated with a single work, Newman's with his *An Essay On the Development of Christian Doctrine* (1845) and Harnack's with his *Wessen des Christentums* (1900), translated into English as *What Is Christianity?*[1] Both men wrote in a period of sharpened consciousness of the historical contrasts between early Christianity and the Christianity of their own contemporary period. So it is that Newman ponders whether first century Christianity is in fact the same as nineteenth century Christianity. Is *A* still *A* or has it become *B*? Harnack asks a similar question: Just what is permanent within the continuing phenomena of Christianity? Each man seeks to answer this issue by means of an historical method. Owen Chadwick has noted that Newman wrote across the top of the original workbooks

---

1. John Henry Newman, **An Essay On The Development of Christian Doctrine** (New York: Doubleday & Co. 1960). Adolf Harnack, **What Is Christianity?** trans. by Thomas Bailey Sanders (New York: Harper & Row, 1957). These two essays are in fact only synopses of each author's views. For further elaboration one should consult Harnack's Prolegomena to his **History of Dogma** (1885) and his smaller work **Christianity and History** (1896). See also Newman's **Grammar of Assent** (1870) and **On Consulting the Faithful in Matters of Faith & Doctrine** (1859).

for his *Essay,* "Tell it historically."[2] Harnack states that he wishes to answer this question "solely in its historical sense."[3]

It would be difficult, if not ludicrous, to claim that either of these two historical methods is free from apologetic especially in light of their denominationally contradictory results. For Newman modern Roman Catholicism represents the fullest explication of the vitality of the Christian "idea." Accordingly, he concludes that the history of Christianity is really the history of Roman Catholicism and not the history of Protestantism. "To be deep in history is to cease to be Protestant."[4] For Harnack, however, the reverse is true. Roman Catholicism represents the full encrustation of the original vitality of Christianity, reflected in the teachings of Jesus, by doctrines and institutional structures. It is Luther in the sixteenth century and Protestantism in the nineteenth century which succeed in peeling away the husk and rediscovering the kernel of Christianity.

In large part these two historical methods are theories about the development or evolution of doctrine. It could be argued that each respective theory offered subsequent generations of Catholics and Protestants apologetic models with which to "historically" defeat the other. However, the main concern at the moment is to compare these theories of development of doctrine as they operate historically to see whence these conflicting results arise. This will be done in two steps: (1) by briefly setting out each theory in comparative fashion and (2) by offering some critical analyses of each theory's methodological adequacy.

To understand the basic structure of Newman's theory of the development of doctrine, one must isolate two lines of argumentation which run throughout his *Essay.* Newman always seeks to determine what is antecedently probable from the nature of

---

2. Owen Chadwick, **From Bossuet to Newman: The Idea of Doctrinal Development** (Cambridge: University of Cambridge Press, 1957), p. 139.
3. Harnack, **What Is Christianity?**, p. 6. For a recent thorough exposition of this work and an assessment of Harnack's critics, see G. Wayne Glick. **The Reality of Christianity** (New York: Harper & Row, 1967), pp. 263-320.
4. Newman, **Essay**, p. 35.

reality *before* he looks for *a posteriori* evidence from history.

Thus Newman's argument normally flows from what is antecedently probable to the historical evidence. On less frequent occasions the reverse can also occur. The normal order of this argument is visible within the structure of the *Essay* itself. In Chapter III, Newman deals with what is antecedently probable in relation to the development of doctrine, and then in Chapter IV looks for historical evidence.

"In all matters of human life, presumption verified by instances, is our ordinary instrument of proof and, if the antecedent probability is great, it almost supersedes instances."[5] Opinions are adhered to "in proportion to the strength of the antecedent probability in their favor."[6] If the historical evidence does not seem to justify such an antecedent opinion, then it may have to be revised.

Newman's entire argument with respect to the development of doctrine proceeds according to the above lines. From antecedent probability it would seem that great ideas are not initially able to be fully absorbed or understood by men's minds. Time and space are necessary for man to come to fully understand such ideas. Thus it is antecedently probable that such an "idea" as Christianity would not be fully understood or explicated within the lifetime of Jesus' disciples. Having posited these probabilities, Newman then goes to history to see whether such development is evident within Christianity. Newman finds that doctrines like the Trinity, Purgatory and Original Sin are not strongly visible in the early church and that they reach lucid expression only in the following centuries. The same is even more radically true for such doctrines as transubstantiation and the seven sacraments.

Newman pursues this line of argumentation with each particular doctrine he treats, e.g., the primacy of the bishop of Rome and the infallibility of the church. The character of creation implies for Newman some necessary provision for the preservation

---

5. Ibid., p. 128.
6. Ibid., p. 117.

of whatever is created. So it is that along with truths of nature there must be some agency for the judgment of these truths, i.e., the human conscience. In parallel fashion, when there are religious truths, it is antecedently probable that there will also be an appropriate agency of judgment and preservation. This would be some sort of infallible authority.[7] Looking to history, Newman sees only one church which has claimed such a status, the church of Rome. It is this analysis/analogy which underlies Newman's observation that "conscience is the aboriginal Vicar of Christ."[8]

In addition to this two part line of argumentation, Newman also makes significant use of historical analogies as part of his method. In general he finds a close correspondence between the past and the present. In 1841 he sees a close parallel between his own situation in England and the Arian controversy. He proposes the following equation: Pure Arians=Protestants, semi-Arians=Anglicans, and Roman Catholics then=Roman Catholics now. Shortly after this, while working on a history of the Monophysites, Newman makes a similar comparison: Eutychians=Protestants, Monophysites=Newman and others, and Catholics at the Council of Chalcedon=Roman Catholics today. In studying Chalcedon, what strikes Newman most is the role played by Leo in determining what became true doctrine. This past situation is quite analogous to Newman's contemporary situation: "I found everywhere one and the same picture, prophetic of our present state, the Church in communion with Rome decreeing and heretics resisting."[9]

---

7. The appropriateness of this authority being infallible is traceable to Newman's assertion that the contrast between these two levels is that between subjective truth and objective truth. Newman, Essay, pp. 103-104.

8. Newman, **Certain Difficulties Felt By Anglicans in Catholic Teaching**, Vol. II (London, 1888), p. 248.

9. Letter, Newman to Mrs. Froude, 1844. For a thorough exposition of how Newman's historical analogies were often quite tied to his own personal situation see Gary Lease, **Newman: Witness To The Faith** (Dublin: Irish University Press, 1971). The above analogies were made in the fallout of his Tract 90. The character of these analogies, in Lease's view, shifts after his conversion to Roman Catholicism, especially after gaining first

In the middle of the twentieth century, especially in the minds of many German and American Catholics, Newman has often been viewed against a liberal backdrop, as one who had aided significantly in the initiation of the discussion about changes within Catholic doctrine. However, to understand Newman properly within his own historical context he must be placed also against the conservative backdrop of the Oxford Movement. When this is done, it may be seen that Newman is fundamentally more concerned to account for the continuity within Christian doctrine and Christianity in the face of acknowledged historical relativities, than to account for the changes themselves. The point is a subtle, but nonetheless a crucial one.

In line with this observation, Chadwick has suggested that Newman's argument in the *Essay* is basically one from immutability. Newman looks for the similarities or resemblances which he senses exist between the early church and the church of his day and, having found such resemblances, he seeks a formal explanation for this.[10] Even though Newman had rejected the *Disciplina Arcani* as well as Vient of Lerins' dictum "Quod ubique, quod

---

hand experience of Roman authority. Thus in the last instance, after the Rambler affair, Newman re-reads the Arians and this time concludes that there must be a distinction made between the **ecclesia docens** (who abandoned the true faith for a period) and the **ecclesia docta** (who held on to the faith and maintained its continuity). Thus his earlier praise of the unrestricted role of the bishop of Rome becomes muted and this role becomes more restricted in the later Roman Catholic Newman.

---

10. The argument is not from mutability but from immutability: "The less mutability has occurred the truer is the modern church; but since history shows that **some** mutability has occurred, even in the least mutable of churches, we need a theory." Chadwick, **From Bossuet to Newman,** p. 144. Cf., Newman, **Essay,** p. 17. Chadwick here implies a three-stage division in Newman's logic: Starting with (1) an a priori, e.g., there will be resemblances between the early church and some church today, Newman moves to (2) the historical data which seems to show a specific church to have such resemblances, and this necessitates (3) an overall theory to explain such mutability. Within Newman's work, however, there is often a blending back of theory into the a priori realm.

semper, quod ab omnibus. . . ," Chadwick views Newman as still using the latter as a norm, if in a somewhat more restricted sense. If Chadwick's position is correct, then there are possible "conservative" ties between Newman and the *semper eadem* of Jacques Bossuet. For Newman, however, unlike Bossuet, variety is not a simple index to unorthodoxy. Nonetheless for Newman Christianity remains fundamentally the same while it is its explication in time and space that develops. Development is explication.

In the *Essay* the "idea" of Christianity seems to be cast in non-relative terms both at its inception, where all is given in Christ, and after the process of doctrinal explication when doctrine is codified as dogma. It is in this middle period or interim process that changes and developments take place in the understanding of Christianity by the human mind as set with different historical and cultural contexts. It is to this middle period that Newman's oft quoted phrase "to live is to change, and to be perfect is to have changed often" seems to have been directed.[11]

Just how the idea of Christianity remains immutable in the face of the process of its explication is evident in Newman's starting point, the Incarnation. In contrast to the low profile Christology of Harnack who starts with the teaching of Jesus, Newman begins with a very high profile Christology, the Incarnaion. This is in keeping with Newman's historical and methodological preference for the writings of the patristic era rather than Scripture. However, Harnack might very well protest that Newman is starting too late and, in fact, starting with a husk rather than the kernel. Harnack regards the equation of Jesus with the Logos as inadmissible.[12]

Newman's argument from immutability may also be evident within the seven principles that he proposes for sorting out proper developments from improper ones, i.e., devolutions. The majority

---

11. Newman, Essay, p. 63.
12. This equation "gave a metaphysical significance to an historical fact; it drew into the domain of cosmology and religious philosophy a person who had appeared in time and space." Harnack, What Is Christianity?, p. 204.

of these principles stress continuity and identity through similarity: "preservation of its type," "continuity of its principles," "anticipation of its future," and so forth.[13]

As was indicated earlier, Adolf von Harnack's attempt to understand change and consistency within Christian beliefs relies in part on the analogy of kernel and husk or on parallel terminology. Harnack views himself as attempting to distinguish not only the kernel of Christianity from its husk, but also its substance from its historical forms, the essential from the phenomenal, and the Gospel within the Gospel from the whole of the Gospel writings.[14]

In order to determine the kernel of Christianity, Harnack suggests a type of method of correlation between the Gospel and the history of Christianity. Accordingly the kernel may be isolated by finding what is common to all historical forms of Christianity and correcting this by reference to the Gospel, while at the same time, in reverse fashion, finding the chief features of the Gospel and correcting these by reference to history. By definition this method of correlation is seen as functioning in both directions.[15]

For Harnack it is impossible to determine what Christianity is if one is restricted solely to Jesus and his teachings. Thus any such quest must include not only the first generation of Jesus' disciples, who were affected by him in their inner life, but also

---

13. The limitation of change and relativity to the explications of Christianity is also implicit in the distinction between real and notional assent as found within Newman's **Grammar of Assent.** J.-H. Walgrave argues that it is this motif which provides the proper interpretative key to understand the **Essay,** even though the latter was written a quarter of a century earlier than the former. In the **Grammar** a dogma is defined as a proposition which can stand either for a notion or for something. If assent is given to the proposition as a notion, this is notional assent or a theological act. If assent is given to that behind the proposition, this is real assent, or a religious act. By implication it is the notional that undergoes development not the reality behind the proposition. Cf., J.-H. Walgrave, **Newman The Theologian** (New York: Sheed & Ward, 1960).

14. Harnack, **What Is Christianity?**, pp. 12-14ff.

15. Ibid., p. 15.

all later products of Christianity as well. "We cannot form any right estimate of the Christian religion unless we take our stand upon a comprehensive induction that shall cover all the facts of history."[16]

However, it is not necessary to wait until the entire course of Christianity has been consulted. The Gospel in the Gospel reveals itself before this because it is

> so simple, something that speaks to us with so much power, that it cannot easily be mistaken.... No one who possesses a fresh eye for what is alive, and a true feeling for what is really great, can fail to see it and distinguish it from its contemporary integument.[17]

In practice the preferred locus for this discovery seems to be the origins of Christianity. "The true perception of what the Christian religion originally was ... alone enables us to distinguish that which sprang out of the inherent power of Christianity from that which it has assimilated in the course of its history."[18]

The Gospel in the Gospel is not a positive religion for it does not contain statutory or particularistic elements. It is religion itself. When Harnack speaks of the teaching of Jesus in *Das Wessen* as (1) the kingdom of God and its coming, (2) God the Father and the infinite value of the human soul, and (3) the higher righteousness and the commandment of love, it might be assumed that these teachings were the substance of Christianity. For Harnack, however, the kernel/husk criterion must be applied even to these teachings. For example, the kingdom of God itself must be distinguished from particular realistic or futuristic interpretations or forms. It should be viewed as fundamentally "the rule of the holy God in the hearts of individuals; *it is God himself in his power.*"[19] In parallel fashion in the third volume of the third edition of the *History of Dogma,* having distinguished three similar sections within the preaching of Jesus, Harnack states

---

16. Ibid., p. 11.
17. Ibid., p. 14.
18. Harnack, **History of Dogma**, Vol. I (3rd ed.; New York: Dover, 1893), p. 39.
19. Harnack, **What Is Christianity?**, pp. 55-56.

that the middle section, dealing with Jesus as Lord, is from "strictly historical and objective grounds . . . the true main section, the gospel in the gospel, and to it I subordinate the other portions."[20]

Ultimately, Harnack, not unlike Newman, views Christianity in personal and relational terminology. In *Christianity and History,* while speaking of what Christianity is, he states that "religion is a relation of the soul to God, and nothing more. That a man should find God and possess Him as his God . . . that is the substance and the aim of religion."[21]The substance of faith "is God the Lord; it is reliance on Jesus Christ, whose word and spirit are even today a witness to the heart and power of God."[22] Thus below all forms, within the teaching of Jesus, lies the Gospel in the Gospel, the reality of Christianity, the relationship between God and man. It is in this sense that Christianity for Harnack is always a question of life enkindling new life, not the handing down of doctrine or statutory elements to the next generation.[23]

In contrast to Newman, Harnack is somewhat pessimistic about the relationship of doctrine to Christian belief. Conceding that Christianity's struggles with nature worship, polytheism, political religions and dualism necessitated the development of new social and intellectual forms, Harnack steadfastly maintains that none of these forms, not even the earliest, can be regarded as possessing a classical or permanent character. They are but bark to protect the tree.[24]

Although admittedly necessary, doctrines and dogmas are nonetheless limitations on Christianity. "Every dogmatic formula is suspicious because it effects a wound on the spirit of religion." This results from the propensity to place dogmatic formulas in

20. Harnack, **History of Dogma**, Vol. III, p. lx.
21. Harnack, **Christianity and History**, trans. by Thomas Bailey Sanders (London: Adams & Charles Black, 1896), p. 41.
22. Harnack, **Christianity and History**, p. 60.
23. Harnack, **What Is Christianity**?, pp. 63, 164ff.
24. Ibid., pp. 190-191.

place of or before religion. "Whatever finds expression in doctrines, regulations, ordinances and forms of public worship comes to be treated as the thing itself."[25] For Harnack this dynamic of the development of doctrine is but the reflection of a universal law of the history of religion: "Religion of strong feeling and of the heart passes into the religion of custom and therefore of form and of law."[26] Chronologically this dynamic effected Christianity in the second century. Ecclesistically this is reflected in the development of the Catholic Church. In Harnack's mind when Christianity succeeded in defeating Gnosticism and other heresies of that period, it actually fell victim to much that it was fighting against: *"Victi victoribus legem dederunt."*[27]

The period of the second and third centuries holds great significance and normative meaning for these two patristic scholars, Newman and Harnack. For Newman it represents the flowering into full classical form such Christian beliefs as Christology and the primacy of the bishop of Rome. In many ways this period is for Newman the high water mark of Christianity. For Harnack this same period holds the opposite significance. This is the period when the Greek notion that "religion is first doctrine" begins to supplant the original, living element within Christianity.[28]

> There is no sadder spectacle than this transformation of Christian religion from worship of God in spirit and truth into a worship of God in signs, formulas and idols. . . . It was to destroy this sort of religion that Jesus suffered himself to be nailed to the cross, and we now find it re-established under his name and authority.[29]

If for Newman this period is the zenith of the relationship be-

---

25. Harnack, **History of Dogma**, Vol. I, pp. 69-70. This is what Tillich would refer to as terminological idolatry.

26. Harnack, **What Is Christianity?**, p. 197.

27. Ibid., p. 207. Marshall McLuhan has taken this dictum and a similar one, "to the victor belongs the spoils," and recast them as a single modern aphorism: "To the spoils belongs the victor."

28. Harnack, **What Is Christianity?**, pp. 208-211.

29. Ibid., p. 238.

tween Christianity and doctrine, for Harnack it is the beginning of the nadir.[30] Full flowering versus encrustation. For Newman the papacy is the necessary analogue to man's conscience, the aboriginal vicar of Christ. For Harnack the rise of the papacy signals the failure of man's individual responsibility. He sums up his view with the French proverb: *"La médiocrité fonde l'authorité."*[31]

In Newman's approach doctrine seems to be tied more intimately to the reality of Christianity than for Harnack. Once a positive doctrinal development occurs, it must be maintained thereafter since it expresses some aspect of the Christian idea. In Harnack dogma tends largely to be associated with a certain period in the past when the Greek spirit strongly effected Christianity, although this tendency toward doctrine and dogma continues. Doctrine and dogma seem to have a more temporary character for Harnack. Thus, while they are needed to meet certain threats to Christianity, after the threat has passed doctrines become disfunctional by tending to be confused with the reality they were designed to express.

For Newman once a doctrine such as the primacy of the bishop of Rome has developed there is no provision for it to go out of style. Thus in Newman's approach there is a certain cumulative effect with respect to doctrines. There is no sense in which circumstances could properly necessitate the reversal of such doctrines or explications once they have occurred. In this way time and historical circumstances for Newman seem to be more an occasion for the development of man's understanding of Christianity rather than the actual cause or determination of the character of this development. For example, in Newman's mind the Incarnation is the *terminus a quo* for the development of

---

30. Harnack does distinguish between the initiation of this encrustation within early Greek Catholicism, where the kernel is still visible beneath the husk, and later Roman Catholicism, where the kernel finds itself fully encrustated and no longer visible. Cf., Harnack, **What Is Christianity?**, pp. 217ff.

31. Harnack, **What Is Christianity?**, pp. 191, 208.

doctrine. Doctrines are seen as the explication of the meaning of the Incarnation. The Incarnation is the archetype of mediation from which flow the doctrines of mediation, such as, the Atonement, the Mass, etc. . . . It is also seen as the archetype of the doctrines of sacramentality, such as the seven sacraments, the unity of the church, the authority of the councils, and so on. Strictly speaking there is no "Gospel in the Gospel" here for Newman. One must either "accept the whole or reject the whole."[32] Thus if Harnack, with his call for "a critical reduction to principle," might be termed a doctrinal reductionist, then Newman might be termed a doctrinal expansionist.

For John Newman the relationship between Christianity and developing doctrine is that of explication and growth. For Harnack this relationship is one of retrogression or entrophy. For Newman the ratio is a direct one, as doctrine develops so Christianity unfolds. For Harnack the ratio is most often an inverse one, as doctrine develops so Christianity is encrusted and incumbered.

In conclusion several critical observations can be made about both Newman's and Harnack's attempts to deal with doctrinal development.

Newman's use of antecedent probability raises several methodological difficulties. Even if it is conceded that antecedent probability does precede historical evidence, the question still remains as to whether this same evidence might just as easily be used to exemplify contradictory antecedent probabilities. For example, if Rome's claims to primacy in the early church can be seen as evidencing the antecedent probability for such a central authority in the church, could not this historical claim just as easily be viewed as evidencing the antecedent probability that power will always attempt to continue its status quo? Thus Geoffrey Barraclough, among others, can argue that Rome's claims to primacy arose in opposition to the counterclaims of

---

32. Newman, **Essay,** p. 111.

Constantinople after the geographical shift of the imperial capital.[33]

Newman may be letting his own view of what is antecedently probable determine not only the interpretation of the facts, but possibly the selection of the facts as well. Of course, it could also be argued that Harnack's model of kernel/husk plays a function quite parallel to that of Newman's antecedent probability. Here we arrive at a familiar question: which comes first the theory/model or the viewing/selection of the data? An adequate historical method would seem to need to include both elements in order to function. The issue may not be so much which is first, as whether there is a constant reciprocal feedback between both elements, each helping to update and correct the other. The point at which either element begins to ignore its partner, may be the point at which the whole procedure becomes suspect.

In this regard two additional points can be made, the first in relation to Newman's knowledge or selection of historical data, the second in relation to Harnack's choice of models.

With respect to the selection of historical data, some Protestant church historians have rightly been criticized for beginning Christian history with the sixteenth century. If they fall victim to historical leaps, so also may Newman. Newman could be criticized for dealing mainly with the first five centuries before jumping into the nineteenth century. This is most evident in the various historical analogies used by him which were noted earlier. Newman's less extensive knowledge or lack of interest in the intervening centuries conveniently allows him to avoid historical data which might have raised havoc with his assumptions. For example, if Newman had been aware of the conciliar tradition in the Middle Ages or the decrees of the Council of Constance, he might not have stated that:

the one essential question is whether the recognized organ of teaching,

---

33. Cf. Geoffrey Barraclough, **Medieval Papacy** (New York: Harcourt, Brace & World, 1968).

the Church herself, acting through Pope or Council as the oracle of heaven, has ever contradicted her own enunciations. If so, the hypothesis which I am advocating is at once shattered; but till I have positive and distinct evidence of the fact, I am slow to give credence to the existence of so great an improbability.[34]

As we have seen earlier Harnack's method, like Newman's, is closely tied to several central analogies. Such analogies at best remain problematic. In Alfred Loisy's famous critique of Harnack's essay, the Catholic Modernist pointed out what a great difference the choice of analogies makes, especially if the analogy chosen is employed as a normative criterion. For example, if one prefers the analogy of seed/tree to that of kernel/husk it would mean that one would not have to unpeel the seed to find out what it is, but rather plant the seed and observe its growth to see what it will bring forth in its maturity.[35] This makes all the more important the basis upon which such an analogy is chosen.

In Harnack's case this choice may rest upon his call for a critical reduction to principle. The issue still remains as to what grounds justify this commitment to this critical reduction to principle or this search for permanence and substance. In short, on what basis does one decide that this critical reduction is the most appropriate model?[36]

---

34. Newman, **Essay**, p. 134.

35. Cf., Alfred Loisy, **The Gospel & the Church**, trans. by Christopher Home (New York: Charles Scribner's Sons, 1912). Newman himself offers the following pertinent observation: "It is sometimes said that the stream is clearest near the spring. Whatever use may fairly be made of the image, it does not apply to the history of a philosophy or sect, which, on the contrary, is more equable, and purer, and stronger, when its bed has become deep, and broad, and full." Newman, Sermon, February 2, 1843, as quoted in Chadwick, **From Bossuet to Newman**, p. 151.

36. Harnack places the burden for doctrinal development, metaphysical reformulations, Gnosticism, intellectualism, etc., largely upon the influx of "the Greek spirit" into Christianity. Without opening a discussion of the accuracy of such an assignment of burden, it might be possible to use this same motif to simply ask whether Harnack's own quest for a critical reduction to principle, the permanent within the transitory, the substance beneath the forms, etc., is itself entirely uninfluenced by this same Greek philosophical concern?

Harnack's aim in the use of this model is to steer a *via media* between two extremes, those who peel everything away until there is no kernel left and those who regard Christianity as identical with a particular historical form. For Harnack it is the Gospel in the Gospel which is permanent and beneath all historical forms. The ultimate criterion which he offers for determining the proper degree of peeling is his reference to men of good heart:

> No one who possesses a fresh eye for what is alive, and a true feeling for what is really great, can fail to see it [the Gospel in the Gospel] and distinguish it from its contemporary intregument.[37]

The question still remains whether the above theologically liberal criterion, i.e., dependence upon men of good heart, is methodologically adequate to the task of the perception of the kernel and the determination of the proper degree of peeling.[38] Further, while Harnack is insistent that no historical form be identified with the substance of Christianity, the very real question remains as to whether the substance of Christianity can ever exist apart from some actual form. To protect against the confusion of any form with the substance of Christianity, Harnack chooses to cut all forms off from Christianity in a quasi-reductionist fashion. Newman, on the other hand, chooses to include such forms in a cumulative development. Neither man, however, offers a final resolution either to this particular question or to the larger debate about the development of doctrine.

---

37. Harnack, **What Is Christianity?**, p. 14.

38. Not only is Harnack's work generally placed within the camp of Protestant liberalism, but this work in particular "has become regarded as the one book which more directly than any other represents so-called liberal Protestant theology." Wilhelm Pauck, **Harnack & Troeltsch: Two Historical Theologians** (New York: Oxford University Press, 1968), pp. 8-9.

CONTRIBUTORS

DAVID H. HOPPER teaches at Macalester College in St. Paul, Minn.

WILLIAM J. HYNES is an Assistant Professor of Religious Studies at Regis College, Denver.

ROBERT G. KLEINHANS is on the theological faculty of Saint Xavier College in Chicago.

BERNARD J. F. LONERGAN of Regis College, Ontario, is the author of many works, including the monumental **Insight**.

FREDERICK R. McMANUS is a professor and dean of the School of Canon Law in the Catholic University of America, Washington, D. C.

WILLIAM E. MURNION teaches religion at Ramapo College of New Jersey, as an Associate Professor of Philosophy and Religion.

JOHN T. NOONAN, Jr., is a Professor of Law at the University of California, Berkeley, and author of such works as the recent **Power to Dissolve.**

BERNARD P. PRUSAK is an Assistant Professor and Chairman of the graduate committee in the Department of Religious Studies at Villanova University, Pennsylvania.

CONRAD SIMONSON is on the religion faculty of Luther College in Decorah, Iowa.

GERARD S. SLOYAN is Professor of New Testament and Chairman of the Department of Religion at Temple University, Philadelphia.

JOSEPH J. SPAE is general secretary of SODEPAX, World Council of Churches, Geneva, Switzerland.

CARL F. STARKLOFF is Chairman of the Religious Studies department at Rockhurst College in Kansas City, Missouri.

AUSTIN B. VAUGHAN is on the faculty of St. Joseph's Seminary, Dunwoodie, at Yonkers in the Archdiocese of New York.

GEORGE DEVINE (Editor) is Chairman and Associate Professor in the Department of Religious Studies at Seton Hall University, South Orange, N. J.